I Remember
SAM SNEAD

I Remember
SAM SNEAD

Memories and Anecdotes of Golf's Slammin' Sammy

MIKE TOWLE

Cumberland House
Nashville, Tennessee

Published by
Cumberland House Publishing, Inc.
431 Harding Industrial Drive
Nashville, TN 37211-3160

Cover design: Gore Studio, Inc.

Library of Congress Cataloging-in-Publication Data
Towle, Mike.
I remember Sam Snead : memories and anecdotes of golf's Slammin' Sammy / Mike Towle.
p. cm.
Includes index.
ISBN 1-58182-326-6 (alk. paper)
1. Snead, Sam, 1912—Anecdotes. 2. Snead, Sam, 1912—Friends and associates.
3. Golfers—United States—Biography. I. Title.

GV964.S6T69 2003
796.352'092—dc21

2002154788

Printed in the United States of America
1 2 3 4 5 6 7—09 08 07 06 05 04 03

To all golfers who have ever called
Richford Country Club home

Contents

Acknowledgments

Thanks to all the following for making themselves available for firsthand interviews for this book: George Archer, Patty Berg, Al Besselink, Tommy Bolt, Johnny Bulla, Larry Dennis, Doug Ford, Mark Fry, Bob Goalby, Freddie Haas, Leonard Kamsler, Gene Littler, John Mahaffey, Gary McCord, Gary Player, Chi Chi Rodriguez, J. C. Snead, Dave Stockton, Bob Toski, Lee Trevino, Jack Vardaman, Don Wade, Lanny Wadkins, Guy Yocom, and Fuzzy Zoeller.

A special thanks to Mark Fry, Bob Goalby, Suzie Snead, and Jack Vardaman for supplying photographs. John Derr was most gracious in allowing me to use two of the anecdotes from his wonderful book *Uphill Is Easier*.

As always, a healthy dose of appreciation goes to the entire gang at Cumberland House Publishing, especially Ron Pitkin, John Mitchell, and Ed Curtis. Cumberland House has taken this series and run well with it.

My wife, Holley, and son, Andrew, patiently waited, and waited, and waited as I worked to get this book finished. Their love and encouragement all along the way were, as always, priceless.

Our friends at Word of Life Fellowship—some old, some new—have added a new and refreshing dimension to our lives.

None of this would be possible without having Jesus Christ in my life as savior, safety net, provider, and protector.

INTRODUCTION

Sam Snead belonged to one of golf's two greatest triumvirates. His threesome was especially noteworthy because all three members were born in the same year—1912.

There was Byron Nelson, the last survivor of the three, a kind, God-fearing man whose eleven consecutive victories and eighteen triumphs overall in 1945 comprise what is generally regarded as the greatest one-year achievement by any golfer.

There was Ben Hogan, a gruff, publicity-fearing man whose career and life were defined by a horrible auto accident, a 1953 season in which he won three majors before skipping the fourth, his entrepreneurial success in starting a golf equipment company, and nearly thirty years of quasi-seclusion before his death in 1997.

Then there was Snead, the outsider, a Virginia hillbilly who had little in common with Nelson and Hogan: Their polar-opposite personalities didn't hide the coincidence that they had practically grown up together as caddies and golfing rivals on the outskirts of Fort Worth, Texas. Snead, Hogan, and Nelson in their prime could have held their own against Nicklaus, Palmer, and Player (or Casper, take your pick), and like their next-generation triumvirate had very little in common with one another. Tour clones didn't exist in those days.

It's harder to define Snead's career because there was so much to it. Like the other two, he turned pro in the early 1930s, 1934 to be precise. Unlike the other two, he was still cashing tournament checks well into his eighties, or more than fifty years after Byron had pretty much retired to his ranch in Roanoke, Texas, and more than a quarter century after Ben had puffed his last cigarette in an official tour event.

Many things come to mind when trying to peg Snead and his accomplishments: the PGA Tour career record of eighty-two official victories (although he, and others, insist that it should number in the high eighties); his amazing athleticism, agility, and suppleness that allowed him to kick eight-foot ceilings as an octogenarian; his winning at Greensboro a tour-record eight times, the last coming at age fifty-three (also a tour record); his never winning the U.S. Open (albeit with numerous close calls); his sweet, silky-smooth swing and the signature Wilson clubs; the straw Panama hat; the outlawed croquet-style putting followed by the sidesaddle technique; his pet fish that lived in a backyard pond; his nearly winning the PGA Championship while in his sixties; and his remarkable play in the early years of the Legends of Golf against "peers" nearly twenty years younger.

The Slammer passed away on May 23, 2002, after suffering a series of ministrokes. Had he lived four more days, Snead would have made it to ninety, just as Nelson had several months earlier. As could be expected, Snead's death elicited the kind of eulogies that typically accompany the deaths of sports legends. Only with Snead, there was no need to airbrush the record or exaggerate it into something it wasn't. One valid debate resurrected by Snead's death was whether he deserved consideration as the greatest golfer of the twentieth century. Yes, he did deserve consideration, but No. 1? Probably not, when considering the likes of Hogan, Nicklaus, Palmer, Jones, and maybe even Tiger Woods on a retroactive exemption. The safest thing to say is that any top three probably should include Snead.

Snead was admired more than he was loved, emulated more than he was embraced. His swing was a thing of sweet tempo and reigned-in power. The older he got, the less he tolerated the sloppy play of amateur partners. But if you shot straight with him regarding your handicap and were willing to risk thirty on a ten-dollar nassau, Snead would more than likely accommodate. He was golf's version of a gym rat, someone who played the game every chance he got and never turned down a challenge to play golf's version of H-O-R-S-E.

When it came to a spot on the scale of public persona, Snead fell somewhere in between Nelson nice and Hogan harsh. Spectators flocked to see Snead, and he signed the occasional autograph. Reporters sought him out for comments and interviews, and he offered up the occasional gem, some of them printable. Those close to Snead laugh off his ribald, risqué sense of humor. Others were turned off. Listen closely enough and Nelson's stomach could be heard turning when Snead got around to telling his dirty jokes at the annual Masters Champions Dinner. Granted, Snead might have been afflicted by the hillbilly shies, and he obviously lacked the P.R. polish of a Nicklaus, Palmer, or Woods, but those who didn't know Snead well were never quite sure what to expect when they entered the conversation zone.

So, why didn't Snead ever win a U.S. Open? Okay, how about Arnold Palmer or Tom Watson never winning the PGA, or Lee Trevino never winning at Augusta, or Nancy Lopez never winning the Women's Open? Ditto for Kathy Whitworth, whose eighty-eight career victories made her the Snead of the ladies' tour. Raymond Floyd won three of the majors at least once each, but never a British Open. Ditto for Byron Nelson.

Sam finished second in the American Open four times. He figured he would have won it seven times had he shot a 69 in the final round those times. Why didn't he win it? Well, there was the eight on the last hole in 1939 when all he needed was a five, or the missed thirty-inch putt in a 1947 play-off. If there was an overall flaw, it might have been his love for his driver and hitting the ball a long way, oftentimes into the notoriously nasty Open rough.

Snead's incredible exploits as a golfer and his uniquely silky swing juxtaposed with his country-boy roots made his life one rich with lore, mostly fact mixed with some fiction. It's true that he had a great-uncle, Big John Snead, who stood about seven and a half feet tall and weighed 350 pounds. Sam's mother was forty-seven when she had Sam, and she had to be in her fifties when Sam saw her deftly handle sacks of flour weighing nearly two hundred pounds. As a high school youth, he could run the hundred-yard dash in ten seconds flat, and at the age of seventy-two he shot a

60 at his home course, The Homestead in Hot Springs, Virginia. The story about him burying money in tomato cans in his backyard probably is false. We think.

I Remember Sam Snead is in no way a comprehensive biography of Snead. It is a collection of a couple hundred or so anecdotes, tall tales, insights, perspectives, and other types of remembrances told, in their own words, by many of the people and peers who knew him best. Consider this a literary scrapbook of one of golf's greatest legends, a man who truly lived a lifelong passion with the game and consistently amazed onlookers with his exploits along the way.

I Remember
SAM SNEAD

1

The Early Years

Sam Snead, born on May 27, 1912, was not cut from the same cloth out of which so many other future golf professionals have been made. He didn't spend an inordinate amount of time working out of caddyshacks, and he wasn't your garden-variety country clubber, born with a silver spoon, or baffy, in his mouth. He was pure country, not country club, from an early age fashioning golf clubs out of sticks and limbs, using stones instead of golf balls while playing a backyard four-hole course with tomato cans as holes.

Young Sam was about seven years old in Hot Springs, Virginia, when he was introduced to real golf. A few buddies from a nearby town invited him to join them for a day of caddying at the local resort club, The Homestead. It was a two-and-a-half mile walk to The Homestead, which in those days was a stroll in the park to the active and athletic Snead.

His first bag that day belonged to a woman who paid him by filling his little cap with pennies and nickels. When Sam got home, however, he was confronted by his angry mom, Laura, who had been searching everywhere for him, not knowing where he was. His punishment was a severe spanking, but it didn't matter. He was hooked on golf and there was no looking back.

Still, it would be years before Sam would devote his time to golf because there was so much else to do in the meantime. In high school he was a multisport star, excelling in basketball, football, and track. He even dabbled in amateur boxing, quitting after one three-round bout. Better he pursue a sport featuring tournaments with four rounds of hitting a golf ball instead of one featuring three-round events with him getting smacked half the time.

In 1934 Snead the golfer turned professional, embarking on a career that in those days necessitated steady work as a club pro. The golf tour was a seasonal distraction that didn't pay particularly well. It required extensive travel that could eat up a roll of bills very quickly. Two years after turning pro, Snead accepted the job as club pro at The Greenbrier in White Sulphur Springs, West Virginia. That same year, 1936, he would also win his first tournament, the West Virginia Closed Professional.

His breakthrough season on what would someday become known as the PGA Tour was 1937, in which he captured the first of his eighty-two official tour victories, the Oakland Open. He also notched his first of four U.S. Open runner-up finishes, signed with Wilson Sporting Goods to play their clubs, and played in the Ryder Cup for the first of seven times.

Playing the tour paved the way for the Virginia boy to expand his horizons and meet golfers and make friends from all walks of life and corners of the country. Strong friendships were forged in the cross-country car rides from event to event, and competitive skills were honed with money games on their days off and during practice rounds.

When Snead started playing golf in his backyard, he often was joined by Homer, a brother twelve years Sam's senior. In fact, it was from emulating Homer and his smooth, long-flowing swing that Sam started to develop the sweet swing that would become one of his trademarks. ***Sam****:*

My earliest memory of golf was when I was seven or eight, and I watched my brother Homer warming up his swing in the cow pasture. I used to shag balls for him. Even so, he didn't pay much attention to me. He wouldn't let me touch his clubs. So I took an old buggy whip and cut it off, then attached an old clubhead to the end. It wasn't anything you might call a club, but, man, you could just sock a ball from here to yonder with it.

One Sunday I whaled a rock through the window of the Baptist Church while the service was on, and that singing stopped awful fast. They never found out who did it, but I was sure *someone* knew. Years later, in 1949, I bought a pipe organ for that church, and only the Lord knew it was my penance.[1]

The backdrop to young Sam Snead's early days as a golfer was the priceless mountainous beauty of Virginia, which provided a natural setting that would serve him well in so many ways. ***Sam****:*

I found that everything I had learned in the woods and around my house could be adapted in one way or another to boost my game. All I did was remember the skills I'd picked up. How to aim. How to slam. How to reckon strategy. How to use psychology on your opponent, knowing that if you didn't go out and get him, he's going to take a bite out of you.[2]

Bob Goalby, *winner of the 1968 Masters Tournament, became one of Snead's best friends and confidantes in the last half of Sam's life. Snead often regaled his younger pal with stories of his past. This really wasn't bragging because, as Dizzy Dean would say, Snead didn't have to exaggerate his many exploits. Goalby recalls Snead's all-around athleticism, which included success in track:*

When he was a junior in high school, he won four events at the state track and field meet. His school won the championship, but it was pretty much because of him. The next year they let him compete in only one event because they didn't want a one-man team dominating the event. That's a shame, because today they would have let him run in everything.

Athleticism and love of sports ran all through the Snead family. Sam's nephew **J. C. Snead** *also turned out to be a multisport overachiever in high school and eventually settled on golf. He was more of a late bloomer, not turning pro until well into his twenties. J. C. is in some ways a chip off his uncle's block, a longtime touring pro who in 2002 won a Senior PGA Tour event at the age of sixty-one. J. C. offers some insights on the Snead family:*

My own dad, Jess, didn't play much golf, although he had played a lot when he was younger, teaming with Sam to take on (brothers) Pete and Homer. You know, the whole Snead family was kind of funny in the way they showed emotion. Especially with Sam and Uncle Homer: They came off kind of hard, as though they put a shield up. They came across as tough, almost mean, but inside they were absolutely the softest, biggest pussies in the world. All of them.

Uncle Homer would do anything in the world for me or anyone he liked, but if he didn't like you, you flat-out knew it. He didn't take any crap from anybody, and he was worse than Sam in that department. Homer had his own range and he would give lessons a lot. I saw him at times just pick up the balls and walk off, saying, "Why don't you just get your ass out of here? You don't want to listen to anything, and I don't have time for this." He was as surly as you could be. But then he would turn right around and go help somebody, even giving them money. It was one way or the other, no in-between.

Sam was a little bit that way, but not as bad as Uncle Homer. Sam could be a little risqué, a little improper at times telling dirty jokes in front of mixed company. Uncouth might be the right word.

When he died, they found out that he had given money to all of the churches in the county. He bought lights for the high school football stadium. He gave the high school scholarship money, and even had the outdoor basketball court paved. He bought organs for the churches. Our high school football team won the state championship last year, and he spent about five or six thousand dollars buying them championship rings. I had a cousin who died from cancer, and I know that Sam must have given him fifteen or twenty thousand dollars cash to help him out in the end, when he really needed it. And he bought his sister a house . . . just all kinds of stuff that people haven't heard about. He didn't want anybody to know about it. He did it because he wanted to do it, not because he wanted somebody to say, "Nice going, Sam." It came from his heart.

There was an old pro by the name of George Lowe, who had the George Lowe putters. George used to hang around on the tour a lot, and he once told me a story that I don't know if it was true or not. I never asked Sam about it because I figured it was none of my business. Porky Oliver was another pro, who would eventually die of cancer. George swore to me that Sam went to see Porky when he was in the hospital, and Sam gave him a blank check, signed. He said, "Porky, I have X amount of dollars. You take what you need."

As good a golfer as Snead was, he remained pretty much a sticks-and-stones guy well into his youth. It wasn't until he turned pro that he got his first set of legitimate equipment. ***Sam****:*

I didn't buy my first set of real clubs until 1934, when I was twenty-two. They were a set of Bobby Jones Spalding irons. It was when they first came out with steel shafts, and I just had to have them. I bought those clubs at five dollars, one club at a time, from the pro (at the Cascades Hotel in Hot Springs, Virginia).[3]

Snead had to work his way up the ladder as a golf pro, and the climb started at his home club in Hot Springs in Virginia, as longtime pal ***Bob Goalby*** *explains:*

Let me tell you how he got his first job as a golf pro. He was from Hot Springs and had grown up at The Homestead, but he later ended up as the pro at Greenbrier.

He was working in the pro shop at The Homestead as a clubmaker, putting shafts in the heads and tightening them. Every year they had to tighten those wooden shafts because they would shrink. They had to take them out and put a roll of string or something around them to tighten them, and then soak them in oil to make them swell up again. That was his job, and he wasn't making peanuts.

One day a woman came into the shop and the shop manager was there. The gal wanted a lesson, but the shop manager said, "I'm sorry, but none of the pros are here right now." She said, "Well, what about that young man over there?" pointing at Sam off to the side working on clubs. The manager said, "He's a clubmaker; he's not the pro." Still, she wanted a lesson. So the manager looks over at Sam and says, "Do you have time to give her a lesson, Sam?" They knew that Sam could play, but in those days the pro sort of held Sam down, not letting him be a part of what they were supposed to be doing because the pros were jealous in those days.

Sam went out and gave this lady a lesson. She really liked what Sam told her and after giving him a little extra tip, she went up and talked to the owner of the place and said, "I just had the finest lesson in my life from a young man today." Two days later, the tennis pro, who was in charge of the whole sports operation at The Homestead, called Sam in and said, "How'd you like to be the pro at the upper Cascades?" referring to the better course of the two at The Homestead. Sam said he about keeled over because that's exactly what he had wanted to do. Be a golf pro. The guy told him, "You'll get a bottle of milk and a sandwich every day; that's your pay, plus whatever you can make (from lessons)." But there weren't many lessons to give because most of the people playing there played the lower course right out the back door.

But Sam got to practice day and night, and he said he got to be pretty good because he got to beat balls. Soon after that they had a tournament for the pros around there, and Sam was leading after the third round. For the last round, the home pro told Sam, "Man, there's no way you can win this tournament with your left elbow flying like that during your swing. How can you play with that chicken wing? You can't beat anybody." Sam said he found out later that they didn't want an assistant pro winning the tournament. Anyway, the pro told this to Sam while walking from the first green to the second tee, and then Sam hit his tee shot halfway up the mountain into the woods on the left. He ended up finishing third instead of winning, and Sam for years would say that he could've killed that guy for what he said to him. It psyched him out because it was clear the home pro didn't want him to win.

Few of Snead's peers from his early days as a touring pro were still around to talk about those early days on tour with Sam. One of those peers still living is ***Johnny Bulla****, who would become Sam's favorite traveling companion for a period of years from the late thirties to the early forties:*

I first met him in 1935 at the Louisville Open. We hit it off real good, right from the beginning. The chemistry just happened to be right.

The big deal in those days was going out to play in tournaments on the West Coast, not so much for the money, but if you played good out there you could get a better job at a club somewhere. We each bought a new Ford in 1936 and decided that when we went to California each year, we would take turns as to whose car we would take. We were big shots then.

We started out by going down to Miami and playing in the Miami Open, and then there was a little tournament in Nassau that we went to. To get there, we took an overnight boat. What it was, was a boat that carried supplies and mail over to the island. It took us most of the night to get there, and the waters were about as rough as they could be. It cost us five dollars roundtrip, and they even served us some dinner on the thing. It was all we could do to hold it down.

I thought I was smart by buying a rope with a big hook on it, and Sam gave me a piece of fish to put on the hook as bait, and I figured I would catch me some fish on the way over. I caught the fish all right, but I got sick pulling it in. Sam comes over and says, "What a fisherman you are. Let me have that." And he took the rope and started fishing from the side of the boat, too. He pulled on the rope a bit and said, "I don't think it's too damn funny," and then he lost his cookies.

We went home for Christmas. After Christmas, he drove down to my house and left his car there, and then we headed out for the West Coast in mine. We drove out together every year until 1942, when I quit to go get my pilot's license. I went to work for Eastern Airlines for four years as a co-pilot. Around this time, Bobby Jones invited me to join his home golf club at East Lake in Atlanta. I ended up playing golf with Bobby at least two or three times a week for three years. But he couldn't really play anymore by then.

After Snead's death in May 2002, ***Bulla*** *wrote a special column for* Golf World *magazine, basically eulogizing a pal who had experienced with him a slice of tour life drastically different from today's world of corporate jets and courtesy cars:*

Those days on the road were something. Wrestling matches in those cheap hotel rooms. Flat tires miles from a gas station. Shooting crows with a .22-caliber rifle to break the boredom as we rode down another two-lane highway. With his great hand-eye coordination, Sam was a heck of a shot.[4]

In an interview for this book, ***Bulla*** *added some interesting details about life on the road with the Slammer:*

Sam was so tight with his money. We would split the cost of gas, and the first time we did it, it was an odd amount and he wouldn't pay the extra penny. I told him, "Tell you what, Sam. From now on, when we stop for gas, I'll give you five dollars and you put in five dollars and you pay for the gas. Then when it's time to stop again, we'll each put in another five and just keep doing it that way." That's the way he manipulated it. Boy, was he tight. But he had a lot of good qualities.

In driving west, we headed toward Texas, and it took us two days just to get across Texas. Then it was into New Mexico and on to Arizona. While we were going through the valley in Arizona, I told Sam, "You know, Sam, this is where I'm going to come back to live later on." He said, "You've got to be kidding." It just hit me. I knew right then that this is what I wanted, and I fell in love with the area. He hated it. Sam had grown up in the mountains with all those hills and trees, and he couldn't see things the same way I did.

For a while after the war, he stayed with me. I had a home about half a block from the entrance to the Phoenix Country Club, where they played the Phoenix Open. Bob Scott, who had been my co-pilot at Eastern, was a general out at Williams Air Base. They had just gotten in some new P-33s, which were the first jet trainers the air force got. Bob said, "Bring Sam out early in the morning, and I'll have the boys give you a little ride, and then after you come back we'll have some breakfast."

When we got out there on the flight line, the pilots were standing there waiting for us. I went up to the pilot that Sam was going to ride with. I said, "You know, I've been a pilot for a while, and he's flown a lot with me, so don't be afraid to give him a fun ride." When we got back after taking the rides, Sam was as green as a gourd and he told me, "You SOB, I'm going to shoot you some day." He wasn't able to eat any of his breakfast because his stomach felt so bad. But he was always pulling stuff on me, too.

One time I played behind him at Pinehurst in the spring North and South tournament, and, of course, he had all of the gallery behind him. Now you've got to remember that I was six-foot-two and weighed about 215 pounds. As I was climbing a hill to the green at one point, he yelled back at me from up ahead, "Boo-boo,"—he always called me that, and I called him "Jackson," because that was his middle name—"you look as big as a bull coming up that hill and almost as smart." He said it as loud as he could, and the whole gallery had a good laugh at my expense.

***Bulla**:*

We drove through all kinds of weather. Sam was a good driver, and I was a good driver, so we never had any wrecks. The agreement we had was that whoever was driving when we had a wreck would pay for it, regardless of whose car we were using at the time. But we never had a wreck, except for a guy that hit me one time.

Another of Snead's running mates from those tour days in the thirties and forties was **Freddie Haas***, now in his eighties, who going into 2003 claimed to be the holder of the longest ongoing streak for consecutive years earning an official tour paycheck, in his case dating back to 1946. Haas talks about how he met and got to know Snead:*

I first met him at the Masters. Charley Yates and I were fortunate enough to find a room for seven dollars a week. It was a wonderful experience to see all of the great players playing in the tournament. At that time Sam Snead was not yet the outstanding player that he came to be. I'm not sure if Hogan was even there.

I really didn't get to know Sam until he started coming through New Orleans in the late thirties. He would come over and visit us at the house, and from then on I got to know Sam pretty good. I think he was the best player that I have ever seen. The only shortcoming I could see in his game was in his failure to manage a golf course. Sam played the way that you should play, but not on the courses where the rough was so horrific that you just handicap yourself one or two strokes.

AP/WIDE WORLD PHOTO

Snead's athleticism was legendary, as displayed here as he leaps over a hedge during the 1937 Metropolitan Open in Bloomfield, New Jersey.

***Haas**, a Louisiana native, on tour life in the thirties and forties:*

Sam would stay with us when he came to New Orleans, and we would have a wonderful time. It was a pleasure to play golf with him, to be able to watch him as well.

Sam was good at a lot of things. For one thing, he could sing. He could also strum a guitar a little. He loved music, and when he came to New Orleans, music was definitely on the agenda. He really had a great time here, going down to the French Quarter to places like Galatoire's and Antoine's.

Wonderful, wonderful food, and then when you got through, you got to experience a little bit of Bourbon Street. But soon it was ten o'clock and you had to tee it up at eight in the morning, so it was time to hit the hay. There was not any of this late-hours stuff, but there was enough time to enjoy the surroundings.

Sam and Jimmy Demaret and Don Cherry, fellows who could really sing, would put on a few shows here and there. When we went down one time to play a tournament in Cuba, Bing Crosby came down, and Bing would get Sam up there and they would harmonize a little bit. It was very interesting, it really was. I couldn't tell you what kind of singer Sam was in terms of being soprano or whatever, only that guys like Bing and Jimmy would enjoy singing with him just a little. Cherry was a professional singer as well as a golfer, and Bing Crosby was no amateur, so when Jimmy got in there singing with those guys, he really needed Sam in there with him to make him sound better. I tried to sing a few notes with them one time, but it didn't take me long to realize that I was out of my element, and so I turned into the best audience that I could be.

There were a few cliques on the tour, but not many. Our problem on tour was sometimes in getting from one place to another. Sometimes we would be in a pretty small coupe with no back seat, and going from New Orleans to Pensacola or Tampa was a pretty good drive. Driving wasn't as easy then because the roads were not as good then as they are now. We didn't fly at all in those days; it was mainly driving the car. With our clubs and all of our luggage, it was usually two to a car, sometimes as many as three, and we would stay together in the same hotel or motel along the way, and that's how we got to know one another.

Plus, we didn't have the social activities that they do now. We played some pro-ams, but not as many as they have now. It was a different environment all the way. It could have been better because we had so much spare time, and on tour spare time isn't really something that you want. Many times our wives were not with us, and then sometimes they were, like when we played down at Seminole Golf Club. On the days between tournaments, we guys would go out and play golf until about four in the afternoon, then come back kind of sweaty, wanting to hit the shower and then maybe rest a bit. But that's when the wives would be ready to have tea and to party.

I made it clear with my wife, Paula, that, "Now look, the thing you've got to do is be out having your fun while I'm out. We just can't have somebody resting over here while the rest of us are out playing, and vice versa. It just doesn't work. We've got to work this thing out." And we did. Paula and some of the other wives then started to get together while we were playing golf, and they got out to go see the world. All I got to see was the golf course and the hotel.

That worked out well for us, but not for all of the golfers. They just didn't work it out, and I'm not sure that Sam and Audry didn't have that problem. She used to travel with Sam, and all of a sudden she didn't travel with him anymore. I don't know what happened. All I know is that when you are on the tour together as husband and wife, you need to have your schedules in sync. If you don't do that, you're missing out. I didn't see Audry on tour after the first few years.

***Doug Ford**, like Bob Goalby, was one of a number of younger golfers who would become good friends with the seemingly ageless Snead. Ford:*

The first time I saw Sam was when I was about sixteen years old. They were playing a 108-hole tournament in Westchester, New York. We sneaked in, and I had played the course quite a few times. The third hole was a par-five, and it had rained for about a week. They had these big ditches to drain the course.

Sam stood up to this par-five, with the green being elevated up on a shelf, and he hit two shots to the middle of the green. I said to the kid walking with me, "I don't know what the hell I'm going to play this game for when he can hit it like that." I couldn't get within a hundred yards of the green on that hole.

I used to kid Sam about why he didn't win all the driving contests. He said to me, "I don't need the money, it's too much trouble." I used to needle him about how long he was, and he used to say to me that the only one who could outhit him was Hogan when the ground was hard and he was hooking it. When Ben first came out he was a low hooker, and his ball would hit the ground and run like hell.

***Bob Toski** came on the golf tour in the early fifties, by which time Snead was firmly entrenched as one of the best golfers in the world. Toski would later become one of the most successful tour players-turned-teachers, instructing the likes of U.S. presidents. Toski's roots were in the tour, however, and he offers a look back to an era in which Snead was battling the likes of Ben Hogan and Jimmy Demaret for tour supremacy:*

Where most of today's tour players are coming out of the college ranks, most of us came out of the caddie ranks. We didn't have the opportunity to play golf in college like they do today. Now they've got tours for kids who are twelve, thirteen, fourteen years old. When I came on tour, the money in tournaments went only twenty players deep. I saw guys leading the tournament only to shoot an 80 on the last day and not make anything. Now that's pressure.

The tour was like a small college fraternity in those days. We had a lot of fun. We didn't discipline ourselves like they do on the tour today. We would raise hell, play golf, raise hell, play golf, and have fun. It's amazing we all played as good as we did. We didn't train like these kids do today, but that shows how talented these guys were back then.

The older guys took a liking to me, I think, because they were sympathetic to me, with my being so small and slight. I wanted to learn. I can't tell you just how much I owe my success in golf to the Sneads, the Nelsons, the Demarets, the Mangrums, the Middlecoffs . . . Ted Kroll, who traveled with me and helped me develop my golf swing. Toney Penna. These guys took a liking to me, and they took care of me.

One of the things we did out on tour that you really don't see much of today is that we helped each other. Today you've got your gurus, your mindbenders, your trainers—all kinds of people. All I know is that I never could afford to pay a guy a million dollars to coach me. We didn't have any money to pay anybody to coach us. There was no such thing as having a swing guru or coach. We pros helped each other because we knew how difficult it was to make a dollar out there, and everybody was closely knit besides. That's what I loved about the tour in the fifties.

We did struggle, but we entertained each other, going out in groups of five or ten. We drank, sang, and had some fun, and we split the checks. Today everybody is very independent and they travel by themselves. They've got their own airplanes, and they get their own suites. Whatever. It's a whole new life out there.

I was successful, and while I never made several million dollars in a year like these guys do nowadays, I wouldn't change a thing from what I did. I'm worth enough money to have security. I wouldn't change the time I had playing golf with those great players for all the money in the world. I'm not knocking the Palmers, the Nicklauses, and all the players that have since come along, but all the money in the world couldn't replace the love and respect I had for those guys back in the fifties, and the love and respect that they had for me.

When Sam passed away, that was a big loss for me, as it was when Demaret left. It's like when (Johnny) Unitas passed away recently. I had several chances to be with him, and he was such a congenial, intelligent, outspoken, wonderful man. I never did play golf with him, but we had some times where we spent talking with each other. You see the beautiful, human side of people that you don't have a chance to do now because everybody is so independent, doing their own thing.

Even though Snead hit his forties in the 1950s, he remained one of the tour's fittest golfers despite what fellow pro **Tommy Bolt** *saw as a drawback in that era when it came to staying in shape:*

You had to take care of yourself in those days. We didn't have one of those fitness trailers running around, following us all around the tour like they do now.

2

THE SWEETEST SWING

Sam Snead might have been the first golfer to personify the game's aesthetic beauty. His swing was an artistic rendering of grace and power, one which *Golf Digest*'s Guy Yocom described as "drenched with honey yet powerful as a trip hammer." Other golfers have had sweet swings but none as consistently productive as Snead's was for so many years.

What set the beauty of Snead's swing apart from all the others were his physique and physical abilities. He was a shade under six feet tall, yet he had the thirty-five-inch arms of someone three or four inches taller. Then there was his incredible suppleness—he could take his ball out of the cup without bending his knees, kick a low ceiling or top of a doorjamb, and touch his fingers to the elbow of the same arm. Many have tried to explain this by referring to Sam's being "double-jointed." His friend Johnny Bulla attributed it to Sam's long tendons and uncommon flexibility.

Whatever the musculoskeletal theories, Snead's swing could play to a metronome. It was the repeating rhythm, the tempo, that made it seem so effortless and which elicited the awe of onlookers. Even when he was in his seventies and eighties, Snead could step onto a practice range and quickly draw a crowd of peach-fuzz pros dropping what they were doing to scurry over and watch, before going back to their practice spot with a waltz-time rhythm humming in their brains. Numerous golfers, Jack Nicklaus included, have admitted that a round of golf with Snead rubbed off on them in the form of an altered rhythm that might stay with them for eighteen or thirty-six holes, or longer. The Sam Snead Fix.

Snead's easygoing swing was not a mistake of nature. He worked on it, for hours on end. He loved different kinds of music and consciously incorporated tunes into his swing's rhythm. He said his favorite was waltz time, or three-quarter time. Merging music with golf was something Snead heard had worked for Bobby Jones. Snead would even whistle a lot on the golf course to help keep his timing and rhythm in sync. Likewise, "Music was and still is a hobby for me," Snead wrote in 1997. "I played several instruments and own a rare Gibson banjo, said to be worth sixty thousand dollars today. I always enjoyed dancing and figured that it helped me to learn and to value rhythm and grace."[1]

***Johnny Bulla** said that Snead was the most natural golfer who ever lived. Not that the game came easy for Snead; it didn't. He worked many long hours for many years sharpening his swing and shotmaking. The natural part was the God-given physical abilities that only enhanced the results of all the hard work:*

People talk about how he was double-jointed. He wasn't double-jointed. There's no such thing. He just had long tendons. He could take his right hand and bend it over and touch his wrist. You think he didn't have long tendons? I've never known anybody else who could do that, besides his having the ability to kick an eight-foot ceiling from a standing position.

He was a great athlete. Those long tendons helped his golf swing because it gave him a longer swing without any added tension. He had a really long swing, and he could wind up his whole body better than anybody. That's why he was so consistent in being able to hit the ball so well.

I could hold my own playing head to head with Sam, whether it was in a practice round or a tournament. But over the course of a tournament and seventy-two holes, I couldn't do what he did because I didn't have the short game.

Tom Watson, *nearly forty years younger than Snead, had no qualms about learning part of the game from the old master:*

He had the best swing there ever was. Of course, I'm prejudiced because my father was a great admirer of Sam's, and he would tell me to watch his swing. I grew up knowing a lot about Sam's swing. I would always go out to the practice tee and watch Sam hit balls, especially when I first got out on tour. Invariably, it would help me to watch him swing. It helped my rhythm and my ability to hit the ball by watching him. I've always had a very quick swing, and by watching him practice I think it smoothed out my swing—at least in my own mind.[2]

***Snead**:*

Swinging the club to a waltz tune is one of my secrets under pressure, and it might just be a good way for you to practice and find a rhythm that works for you.[3]

Snead admitted that much of his yearning for nice tempo and rhythm in his swing came from watching Bobby Jones, whose 1930 Grand Slam, or "Impregnable Quadrilateral," still is considered one of the greatest achievements in golf history. ***Bob Goalby****, a close friend of Snead, explains the Jones influence:*

Sam told me that Jones was one guy who had two "speeds" on the par-fives. He was long. He could play the big swing and hook out there and get another twenty-five yards. That's pretty difficult for the average player to do, but he had that smooth, easy swing. Whenever he had to, he could wind it up a little bit more and hit it even harder. Snead himself said that he only ever swung at about 80 percent, and that it was something he had learned from Jones. He played a few rounds with Jones in the thirties, and saw how smoothly he swung and how far he could hit it, and that helped him. Snead had that rhythmic swing anyway, and maybe his seeing Jones play just cemented it.[4]

See what ***Sam*** *himself had to say about his own swing:*

I try to get "oily." . . . Oily is the opposite of jerky. You know, if a baseball pitcher has a herky-jerky motion, he won't last long. Oily means a *smooth* motion. It's the feeling that all your bones and muscles are so in sync, any movement you make is gong to be smooth and graceful. Your mind will make a million little corrections as you swing, and it'll be happening way too fast for you to worry about. All you need to do consciously is to be the maintenance man, keeping the works good and loose and *oily*.[5]

Legendary swing sage **Harvey Penick**, *whose* Harvey Penick's Little Red Book *became a runaway bestseller, made this observation about Snead's swing:*

I remember someone asking to see the calluses on Sam Snead's palms. Sam said, "I don't have any calluses." Sam said he holds the club as if it is a live bird in his hands, with just enough pressure that the bird can't fly away but not so tightly that the bird can't breathe. Grip the club this way and you won't have calluses, either.[6]

Golf writer **Dick Aultman** *explained Snead's swing in an article titled "A Swing for All Ages":*

Snead's swing is probably best known for its unhurried, flowing grace. It gives this appearance largely because it is so unified. When he came on the scene in the 1930s, the emphasis was still on "hand action." While Sam certainly does nothing to stifle normal use of his hands, his swing exemplifies the "one-piece" unification of body, legs, and arms. His arms swing back and up in direct conjunction with the turning of his body. There is absolutely no independent lifting or turning of the club with his hands and wrists, no flippiness at the top, no casting with the hands at the start of the downswing. In short, his hands are "quiet" throughout his swing. It is this lack of wristy jerking above all else that makes Snead's swing look so smooth. It is also a major reason for his remarkable consistency over the years.[7]

***Snead** said he rarely swung the club as hard as he could:*

I've always tried to swing at about 85 percent of my top speed. That's a pace I can control, and by swinging a little slower and smoother, if I do miss the shot, at least I have a fighting chance of recovering and saving par. If I haul off and try to powder the ball, I might hit the shot off the world, and it doesn't take too many mistakes like that to send you down the road.[8]

*Although **Snead** almost always had an extra gear or two he could go to in his swing, he was as likely to slow it down even further than to speed it up:*

As hard as it may seem to understand, when I really wanted to hit it a long way—say, in a driving contest or a par-five without any out-of-bounds—I would try to swing slower, not faster. I heard Jack Nicklaus say this when he came up, too. I would try to make a bigger turn by going a little slower. When I went slower, I felt I could get the club into a good position and return it square to the line I wanted the ball to travel on.[9]

Tommy Bolt:

I would compare Sam to Joe DiMaggio. The beautiful swing, the nice tempo. DiMaggio had good tempo. Ted Williams, too. Those two.

Jack Vardaman, *a Washington, D.C., attorney, met Snead soon after buying a second home in Hot Springs in 1980. Vardaman is a scratch golfer, and it wasn't long before he started hooking up with Snead for lots of golf games at The Homestead:*

Sam was a hero in a classical sense. That is, he was someone who could do heroic things on the golf course. In addition to his unequaled record of tournament wins, he would do things that, when people saw them, they would sort of become legend.

Anyone who played the tour with Sam when he was in his prime will tell you that he was the best shotmaker ever.

J. C. (Snead) told me the story of being on the first tee one time with a new driver, a big wooden-head driver. Sam was playing in the tournament, and Hale Irwin was there as well. They were looking at this driver, and Hale said, "That's a good-looking driver, but you could never hit that off the deck." Sam said, "Let me see that." He takes the club from J. C. and says, "I think I could hit this ball off the deck and over that big oak tree out there." Hale said, "You do that, and I'll go pick it up." Sam took that driver, dropped a ball on the ground, and sailed it right over that big tree. He turned to Hale and said, "There it is, son. Now go pick it up."

Another thing I remember is a story I heard Nick Faldo tell. When Faldo was a teenager in England, Sam was over there giving an exhibition. Nick and a number of his schoolmates were watching. After a while, Sam had gone through all the clubs in the bag and was down to the driver. Spectators were calling shots for him, and Sam was hitting the shots they called.

Finally, he put a ball on the ground, and they said, "Okay, let's see you hit a high cut off the ground."

Sam hit a high cut.

"Let's see you hit a low draw off the ground."

Not a problem.

Then they said, "Let's see you hit a low cut."

Sam had no problem with that, either.

Finally, they said, "Is it possible that you could hit a high draw off the deck with a driver?"

Sam hit the ball. It sailed as high as you could want it, with the gentlest little draw, at which point Nick turned to his friends and said, "Let's go, mates. We've got work to do."

He could hit a shot out of a bunker and make it bounce once or make it bounce twice—whatever he wanted.

Sam wasn't just better than the people he played against, but like the greats of any sport, he was really different. This was somebody who was one of the greats in golf history, not just somebody who had won a lot of tournaments. He could do things on the golf course and do things with a golf ball that others couldn't do. He wasn't just better, he was light years better. He could make the seemingly impossible look effortless.

A lot of people are given gifts—it's what you do with them that matters, and he did a lot with his.

Vardaman:

I played golf with him over the years up to the time where he didn't play much because his eyesight had gotten so bad. He would still hit balls every day, and I would generally try to time my practice time so that I would be on the practice tee with Sam.

When I had first met Sam and we started playing, he would never give any instruction unsolicited, and he wouldn't give you much solicited. Toward his later years, however, Sam loved to help people with their golf game. He would talk about swing thoughts and what was important and what was not important. He would make it sound simple, but if you probed him a little, he understood and could explain all the complexities of the golf swing.

People sometimes think that Sam had this natural, God-given swing and that he didn't know much about the swing because he talked about it in rather simple terms. In fact, Sam's "natural" swing was the product of an extraordinary amount of work and effort. It looked natural because he developed it so well. He practiced all the time.

One of the first tips he gave me was when he said, "You look at most of the good tall players"—I'm six-two—"they keep their left foot on the ground when they take the club back. Your lower body moves a little too much, so let's try keeping your left foot on the ground." That tip helped me a great deal, especially in consistency.

Doug Ford, *winner of two majors, the 1955 PGA Championship and the 1957 Masters, said Snead's great swing worked for all of the clubs in his bag:*

AP/WIDE WORLD PHOTO

An excellent baseball player as a youth, Snead doesn't look entirely out of place in laying down a bunt in a pregame exhibition before a 1954 game between the New York Yankees and Washington Senators at Griffith Stadium.

No one ever swung the club as smooth and as perfect as Sam did, and he worked hard on his game. *Golf Digest* used to send out a poll each year asking every player to name who they thought was the best player for each club in the bag. We would just write "Sam Snead" across the whole thing and send it back.

You could say that even with the putter. He was a super putter until he got the yips. If they had allowed him to keep putting croquet-style, he would really have had some record in those years that they barred it. They (the USGA) ended up allowing the long putters to be used, when I would think that the croquet style is closer to being in line with the spirit of the Rules of Golf than the long putter is. At least with the croquet style, you're using standard equipment. They didn't like it when he went to the sidesaddle, although they couldn't say anything against it.

Lee Trevino *explains why it would be a mistake to let memories of Snead's game fade away:*

Unfortunately, I don't think today's generation of golfers really knows much about Sam Snead. What a phenomenal golfer. He really knew how to play the game, and it was amazing what he could do with a golf ball. His was the sweetest golf swing I had ever seen. Some people were quick to criticize that he went too far inside on the way back, and it looked like he went over the top of the ball. But, actually, he didn't go over the top of the ball. His shoulder may have looked like it went over, but his hands were in perfect position down in the hitting area.

His backswing reminded me so much of what little I've ever seen of Bobby Jones's backswing, by taking the club back so much inside.

And Sam was strong—very agile, so supple. I remember him standing in the middle of a room when he was like sixty-four or sixty-five years old, and looking over at me and saying, "Hey, hey, hey-hey." And I said, "What is it, Sam?" And he just looked up at the ceiling, where there was a light bulb plugged into a light socket, and all he was trying to do was get everybody's attention. I would play along and say, "Now Sam, don't you go kicking that light bulb!" At that, everyone would turn to watch. Keeping his left foot on the ground, Sam kicked his right leg up, and he was so agile that he could kick the light bulb out on the eight-foot ceiling.

He was born with the gift, being so supple, and that's exactly how he swung the golf club. But no, he wasn't double-jointed—there's no such animal. He was just a very supple guy.

There never will be anyone to replace Sam Snead, just like there will never be anybody to replace Hogan. You can compare golfers and say who was better than whom and all that stuff, but when you analyze it and dissect it—as also was the case with Byron Nelson winning eleven tournaments in a row—you realize that each of these guys was one of a kind. There's Hogan coming back after the bus accident that nearly killed him and winning all those majors, and then there's a guy like Arnold Palmer who muscled the ball around without a lot of finesse, and people loved it.

Today you've got guys with all this new technology hitting the ball three hundred yards and people go "Wow," when in fact those older guys were hitting it over three hundred yards decades earlier. The technology really doesn't make the difference. Take those guys from thirty-five to forty years ago and give them all the stuff guys are using today, and those guys would have been hitting it even farther than the guys of today do. You just can't believe how hard and how fast those guys were able to swing the club.

Look at Nicklaus—he was hitting the older ball over three hundred yards with a forty-three-inch steel shaft and a wooden head. Arnold Palmer could also hit it long. But no one was as long as George Bayer. He could fly it past Jack Nicklaus's ball. Just think what those guys, in their primes, could do today. So when you talk about Tiger Woods hitting the ball umpteen million miles, we had the same kind of guys back then, and that included Sam Snead.

***Harvey Penick*:**

People would say Sam looked like he was aimed to the right. Playing at the Masters one time, another player told him, "Sam, you are aimed at my caddie." Sam said, "No, I'm aimed at my own caddie."

For Sam, the aim was perfect. He aimed a little to the right and hooked it.[10]

Penick, *again:*

Sam hit that low, bullet-type shot. If you want distance—whether it's for a shot-put, a BB gun, or a cannon—you would want to launch at about a forty-five-degree angle. That's what most of us try to do.

But Sam hit down on the ball a little bit to get that bullet flying. For this reason, he used a driver off the tee with the loft of a brassie.[11]

Jack Nicklaus *was seventeen years old when he got to play with Snead for the first time. In between rounds of the 1957 Ohio Open, Nicklaus made a side trip via private plane to play alongside Snead in an exhibition. It would be the first time that a young Nicklaus would play a golf round in front of thousands, and he was nervous. Nicklaus:*

Still sharp in my mind is how hard I found it to concentrate on my own game during our match. All I really wanted to do was study Sam, watch that big, beautifully flowing golf swing and the wondrous drives and iron shots that poured from it so effortlessly. If memory serves, I shot 72 and Sam 68. Apart from calling me "Junior," he could not have been nicer, and I had a fine old time with him.

And, of course, like everyone else who's played with Sam Snead, I tried to copy him, particularly his tempo. Gradually, as the round progressed, my aggressive lash at the ball became magically transformed into a carbon copy of history's all-time smoothest and most graceful golf swing. At least, that's what happened in my mind. And, in truth, enough of

Sam's rhythm rubbed off to make me at least temporarily a better player, because the next morning at Marietta (at the Ohio Open) I went out and shot an almost flawless 64, then won the championship with a 72 in the afternoon.[12]

Golfer **George Archer**, *still active on what is now known as the Champions Tour, recalls a time in the early seventies while practicing and getting ready to play at Greensboro that he was approached by Snead, who had a favor to ask:*

When I won Greensboro the second time, they didn't have a driving green. I was in the tenth fairway hitting balls across the fairway up onto this lady's lawn. My caddie was up there shagging balls for me. Along comes Sam, and his caddie wasn't there.

It was a two-tee start. I had a 7:12 time and Sam something like 7:04 or 7:05—they started at something like 6:30 in the morning in those days to get the two rounds in. It's about quarter to seven, and Sam runs up to me and says, "Hey, George, my caddie isn't here yet, but I need to hit a few balls to warm up. Let me hit some of your balls—where's your caddie?" There were a number of caddies out there in people's nearby yards shagging for their golfers, and we could only use up to about a seven-iron because we only had about 150 yards to work with.

I said, "Sam, you're going off ahead of me. Why don't you just step in here and hit up to that kid up there?" while I pointed out my caddie to him. Sam stepped into my spot and hit a few shots. I said, "Hit a couple balls with your driver if you want," the idea being that you would hit some drives off over some trees out of the range of the caddies and the people's yards.

He lost some of my balls, sure, but I stole his tempo right there. I just sat there for a number of minutes watching his rhythm. So after he left and went over to the tee, I stood up and just saw that rhythm in my head, and I hit a few more shots. I remember walking over to the first tee—and I had thirty-six holes to play that day—and just had a clear picture of his rhythm when I got up there to tee the ball off. I said to myself, *Now you're Sam Snead, just make that swing.* And I went on to win the tournament. That's something I'll always be grateful to Sam for, but I was also smart enough to recognize that he had the greatest rhythm of anyone who ever swung a club. That rhythm stayed with me the whole day.

A lot of times over the years I would purposely go over to the practice tee and try to be next to Sam while hitting balls, trying to steal his rhythm because it worked. It helped me. I also played with Hogan several times, including in my first U.S. Open, but you couldn't steal Hogan's rhythm. It was too fast for me. It was so quick through the ball that it wasn't a rhythm that I could visualize. But the way Sam swung, I could visualize that and steal it—if you want to call it stealing. Perhaps a better word is "copy."

***Chi Chi Rodriguez** can remember playing a lot of rounds with Snead but can't remember any times when it was Snead paying off the bet at the end of the round. Rodriguez ended up paying, which he saw as a cheap investment in his own game:*

Sam gave me a lesson on the Skins game in Hawaii. I asked him if he could help me out with my swing, and he said, "What swing? You never had a swing."

I would play him and always lose twenty dollars to him,

but, hey, what's twenty dollars for playing four, four and a half hours with Sam Snead? That's the cheapest lesson a man could possibly have.

He was the best player I ever saw, although Tiger Woods is coming close to him now. Tiger can move the ball, too, but we are playing with different equipment now. When Bobby Jones was asked about Jack Nicklaus's game, he said, "That young man plays a game with which I am not familiar."

I think Sam Snead was the *best* player I've ever seen in my life and Jack Nicklaus the *greatest*, but Tiger is getting ready to come through. Tiger is the first guy I've seen without a weakness. I could beat Jack Nicklaus out of the traps; I could drive the ball better than Gary Player; I could hit better trap shots than Arnold Palmer; and I could hit the right club more often than Sam Snead. I don't see any part of the game that I ever could have beaten Tiger Woods at, and that bothers me. He's the whole package.

J. C. Snead, *Sam's nephew, didn't really get to know his famous uncle until he was well into his twenties and a newcomer to the PGA Tour, but the ice between them eventually melted. In time, Sam was helping his nephew with his swing, and much more:*

Sam helped me a lot with the mental part of the game, too. Like, you don't need to hit a nine-iron 160 yards. It's better to hit the ball 125 or 130 yards with the nine-iron and learn how to play well within yourself.

I watched him all the time and tried to emulate what he did as far as hitting shots—when to hit it high, when to hit it low, when to hit it right, and when to hit it left. Or knock it down—just how you maneuver the ball. And that's how I really learned how to play golf, just by watching him.

After I got out there, I played my first three years with all the other rabbits, trying to make it by from week to week. Finally, I won a tournament and found myself getting paired with some of the big-name guys. That's when I found out I could hit it better than a lot of them could. Literally. I could strike the ball better because I just fashioned my swing after Sam's, and I had figured that everybody that's a good player just plays that way. I hadn't realized that I had been watching a Picasso the whole time. I figured that now that I was playing with the big shots, I would see some really good stuff. But what I found out was that I was just as good as they were. It was almost shocking to me. I could hit the ball better than they could, although they were able to manage their games and putt better than I could.

Over the years you hear people talking about all these hotshots, but after you've seen Sam, you realize that all these other guys don't really know what playing is all about. I'd like to see some of these hotshots hit a driver up over a tree off the ground, or hit a soft, high-cut one-iron and stop it within a yard of landing, or hit a boring driver that goes out there head-high and then draws and runs about a hundred yards into the wind. I don't see anybody doing that today. Everyone is playing straight golf. Of course, the equipment today has really forced you to be that way. It's really hard to maneuver the golf ball because they have all these dimples that make the ball correct itself in flight.

***Al Besselink**, another veteran golfer who joined the tour about a decade after Snead did, was one of the most popular* *players in his day. He often gravitated toward Snead to see what he could pick up, both in terms of the golf and the stories:*

Sam Snead was one of the greatest guys I ever met in my life. He was one of the funniest guys in the world and would never do anything to try and hurt you. When you were playing in a tournament, he wouldn't do anything to upset you or your golf game.

I must have played five hundred rounds of golf with Sam Snead and guys like Doug Ford, Bob Goalby, and Jerry Barber. There were times that we might play fifty-four holes on a Monday or Tuesday. We'd go round and round and round playing ten-dollar nassaus. In our day, you didn't win much money on the tour unless you finished in the top five, so all we would do was bet and gamble on the other days.

Sam was the greatest swinger of the golf club there ever was. He could take that club and do things that were unbelievable. If we had had the greens they do today . . . he would have won two hundred tournaments. He would have been the Tiger Woods of his day, and I think Tiger Woods is the greatest thing that has ever come along on the golf course.

Just playing alongside Snead was an experience to relish. Every time a big tournament came along, I would try to play at least one practice round with Snead and Hogan. First of all, you had the big gallery and you were playing in a match even though it was just a so-called practice round, and I was tight because there was a lot of pressure. But that was great preparation for the actual tournament. Plus all the media would be there—the writers and the photographers. They'd come out to catch Snead and Hogan, and I would be right in the middle of them. So the next day I could see my picture right in the middle of the newspaper.

Then I'd tee off early Thursday morning with two other guys, and it would just be us three with our three caddies going around the course by ourselves. I had had my tournament the day before, so this was easy by comparison. That's why I finished in the top eight in the Masters three straight years, third in the U.S. Open at Oakland Hills in Detroit, and tenth in the Open at Merion. I attribute all that to a guy like Sam Snead. To play a round of golf with Sam Snead was truly special. He had the most fluid, beautiful golf swing God ever gave anybody.

I loved to be around Sam Snead, and not just because of being able to watch him swing a golf club up close. I remember his shooting 28 or 29 (for nine holes) against me a few times without making a putt. He loved to grab that ten dollars or that forty dollars, or whatever the bet was, and that was his piece of pie. He loved to play and he was a competitor.

Few tour players have ever been as able to break down the golf swing as well as ***Bob Toski*** *can. Much of his swing expertise was acquired through the power of observation. With Sam Snead, he had the perfect subject to study:*

I first met Sam when I started full time on the tour in the fifties. I think one thing a lot of people don't fully appreciate or understand about Sam is that he was, as we all know, a very homespun Virginia hillbilly. I think he's the only guy who ever played a practice round at Augusta in bare feet. He always said that if you know how to play golf, you can always find your balance through your feet; you don't need spikes. A lot of people will say that you "control action through traction," but balance is controlled through your feet. If you take your golf shoes off and try swinging in your bare feet, you'll find out in about two seconds how much control you have of your body.

Sam and I, with me as a teacher, had a lot in common in the simplistic way that we taught golf. He was very sensible in his approach to teaching golf. Sam didn't have the great control of the language that other teachers might have had, but he would certainly get his message across in a very simple and practical manner. He understood the swing from an orthodox standpoint because his own swing was an orthodox swing.

Sam had the best-looking swing in golf that I have ever seen in that he swung a golf club with the three things that I have always felt are applicable to a good swing: He had a swinging force, a turning force, and a shifting force. There's an old saying in teaching golf that goes way back, and it says, "Great players swing beautifully above the waist, and move beautifully beneath the waist." One teacher, I think it was Seymour Dunn, said that most golfers do neither. Sam did both, and his swing looked effortless because of what he did with the three motions with the swing, turn, and shift. He controlled those three parts to where he had effortless power, where most people have powerless effort.

Some people have said that Sam had a one-piece swing and it may have appeared that way, but if you had a one-piece swing, you would have no wrist cock, like a pendulum in a clock—a one-lever swing. You need to create an angle because that's the only way to get the club to parallel in the backswing. But the putting stroke is a one-piece swing.

Tommy Bolt*, winner of the 1958 U.S. Open, admitted to being another of the many golfers who benefited from playing*

PHOTO COURTESY OF BOB TOSKI

Bob Toski and Sam Snead: two men whose knowledge of the golf swing has been among the best in the world.

a round or two with Sam Snead, an experience which could be compared to recharging the batteries:

Sam could play all the shots. He could hook the ball or fade the ball at will. And his tempo was the greatest.

Right before I won the Open at Tulsa, I missed a four-foot putt at the last hole in Dallas to get into a play-off there with three or four others. Snead birdied the first hole of the play-off and won the tournament. The next week, I played two practice rounds with Sam at Tulsa. I developed some good tempo off of him. That's the reason I won the tournament, because I concentrated on tempo and keeping within myself.

I went to the next tournament, the Buick Open in Flint, Michigan, and led through the first three rounds there, only to finally lose it the last day when I got tired. That's my excuse anyway—I lost my concentration and (Billy) Casper won the tournament. I shot 74. All told, I had led the U.S. Open all four rounds and then the Buick Open for the first three rounds, so that's seven straight rounds in which I held the lead, and holding the lead that long will wear on anybody. I finally wilted and they went by me.

Guys loved to play practice rounds with him, and Sam liked to gamble a little bit. We would play ten- and twenty-dollar nassaus all the time.

Bob Toski:

I've always felt that the tempo of a golf swing was in the rhythm of the arms in allowing the rhythm of the body to keep pace. You see, your hands and wrists have a lot of speed, and if you get handsy and wristy, then your rhythm is off. It's like when you walk. If you swing your arms as you walk, you will have a gait and rhythm that looks right. However, if while walking, all you do is turn and snap your wrists and twist your shoulders, you don't have any rhythm.

I'll put it very simply. I believe in the theory that if you have a free, smooth arm swing, this is the essence of what makes your golf swing look like Sam Snead's. He had a beautiful, rhythmic arm swing with the lead arm in control of the backswing because it was the straighter of the two levers. The right arm would bend to support the left arm, but Sam would control the speed and the ratio of the length of his arms in such a way that his backswing looked rhythmic and effortless. Then he complemented that by allowing his body to turn in rhythm with his arm flow. That's the secret to a rhythmic, controlled swing—to have the free, unforced arm swing, not a forced arm swing, not a forced hand swing, not a forced body turn.

Sam always said that the golf swing is a measured time, which few people have ever learned to pace. He gave the length of his arms and the turning of his upper chest and body time to set the club into position. And then down he went.

3

Playing in the Majors

Sam Snead accomplished a lot of things and he won a bushelful of tournaments, but he never won a U.S. Open. That gap in his record will remain a part of his legacy forever. With anyone, there's always something to quibble about. But without a U.S. Open trophy in Snead's closet, the argument can always be made that it's difficult to call him the greatest golfer who ever played, because he never ever was able to win our national championship.

There were a number of close calls. Snead himself once counted up seven American Opens that he would have won had he only shot a 69 in the final round.

Two Open close calls stand out from all the rest. The first was in 1939, when in the last round he triple-bogeyed the par-five eighteenth at Philadelphia Country Club and missed, by two strokes, making it into a play-off that ultimately was won by Byron Nelson. They didn't have scoreboards in those days, and Snead went to the eighteenth thinking he needed a birdie four to win, when a par five would have sufficed. After hitting his drive into a fairway bunker, he played too aggressively trying to get close to or reach the green in two, when a lay-up would have been the right strategy.

Then, in 1947, Snead missed a thirty-inch putt on the eighteenth hole of a play-off at Saint Louis Country Club to lose to Lew Worsham. It didn't seem to matter that Snead had made an eighteen-footer in regulation to force the play-off. His short miss at eighteen in the play-off sealed his fate and gave rise to the ridiculous premise that maybe Snead hadn't been such a great putter after all. Gamesmanship might have been a factor: Snead's miss came after a brief delay in which Worsham called for a measurement of their respective remaining putts, delaying Snead's chance to putt out after his long first putt had missed.

Snead was runner-up in three other Opens: in 1937, two shots behind winner Ralph Guldahl; in 1949, tied with Clayton Heafner, one stroke behind Cary Middlecoff; and in 1953, six behind Ben Hogan.

Snead won a total of seven major titles—three Masters Tournaments (1949, 1952, and 1954), three PGA Championships (1942, 1949, and 1951), and a British Open (1946). Interestingly, as many years as Snead played tour golf, and with his first and last tour victories spanning thirty years (1936–65), all of his major triumphs were clustered within a thirteen-year stretch, with six of those grouped within a nine-year stretch. What does that say? Perhaps it is that, while Snead probably played better golf longer than anyone else in history, his best golf had a comparatively short shelf life.

Of all his major victories, his most memorable had to be his 1954 win at Augusta. He bested his rival Ben Hogan by one stroke in an eighteen-hole play-off. Snead's most unexpected major win probably was his British Open title in 1946. He went overseas to play in it only at the prodding of his good travel buddy, Johnny Bulla. Then while riding in a train to get to the course, Snead looked out the window and saw what appeared to be a golf course, with its falling fences, spotty turf, and apparently unkempt bunkers. He turned to a passenger seated next to him and said, "What abandoned golf course is that?" The golf course he had dissed turned out to be the venerable St. Andrews Old Course in Scotland, the site of that year's British Open. Snead ended up winning by four shots over Bobby Locke and, yes, Bulla.

Speaking of ***Johnny Bulla****, he had a front-row seat to some of Snead's U.S. Open woes:*

I was paired with Sam in a lot of the Opens, so I was able to see much of what he did or didn't do. If he would have driven the ball as well as I could, he could have won six or seven Opens. I know he would've.

The way Phil Mickelson plays reminds me a lot of the way Sam played. Phil hits a lot of great shots, but he also hits too many balls from the rough, and you can't be doing that to win the Open. You've got to hit your driver well all the time, unless you have the strength of Tiger Woods.

We all have our destiny, and Sam's included not winning the U.S. Open. I'm a believer in that. But truth be told, Sam never drove the ball straight enough to do as well as he could have in the Open. He hit too many bad drives, and the high rough slowed him down just enough. If you hit a drive into that rough, three out of four times you're going to end up with a bogey. Nowadays, guys can advance the ball over a hundred yards from the rough, but we couldn't do that in our day.

When he took that eight at the last hole of the Philadelphia Country Club (in 1939), he had driven into the rough and then taken a three-wood out because he thought he needed a birdie four to tie (clubhouse leader Byron Nelson). He hit it well, but it came out low and buried in a trap short of the green. Now he had no shot at all, and he ended up with the eight on the hole.

What was kind of funny about the whole thing is that I had been leading after fifty-four holes with the lowest three-round score that had ever been shot in an Open up until that time. But I had a bad last round. Sam and I ended up having dinner together that night. We went the whole meal without saying one word about that last round. What was there for either one of us to say?

I felt I got snookered out of my chance to win. I played the last round with Ralph Guldahl, who had won the two previous Opens, and I felt he did everything he could to mess me up. And he did a good job, sometimes just saying things. At one point I was standing over a five-foot putt at the tenth hole just getting ready to hit, when Ralph came up to me and said, "Do you know which way that's going to break?" He told me it was going to break right, and it ended up breaking to the left about a foot, and I missed it. A few other times when I was over short putts, he would move when I started to putt it.

I think his never winning the Open bothered Sam every day of his life, even though he would talk around it. Instead of enjoying what he accomplished, he would always be worried about something he couldn't have or didn't get. He said to me, "Boo-boo, there isn't a day that passes by that I don't think about not winning the Open."

PHOTO COURTESY OF BOB GOALBY

Perhaps never winning the U.S. Open affected Snead enough to where he started effecting unorthodox putting styles, such as the sidesaddle.

Snead *had this to say after his final-hole eight cost him a chance at the 1939 Open in Philadelphia:*

That night I was ready to go out with a gun and pay somebody to shoot me. It weighed on my mind so much that I dropped ten pounds, lost more hair, and began to choke up even on practice rounds.[1]

As for his never having won the U.S. Open, period, **Snead** *finally zeroed in on what he thought his problem to be:*

Oh, I've blamed it on the crowd, on the pain in my back, and everything else. But thinking about it all these years I've come to the conclusion that my enemy going into the Open was my own publicity. My early wins and the way the papers whooped me up made me too damned cocky.[2]

***Snead**, once again on his Open-less résumé:*

Did never winning the Open bother me? Of course it did, although I always figured that it was predestined. I just wasn't meant to win the Open. It was as though the man upstairs said, "Sam, we gave you a lot, but we're not going to let you have a full plate." So be it, but it has caused me some restless nights of tossing and turning.[3]

*Veteran tour golfer **Al Besselink** said that to this day he still can't fully fathom that Snead never won a U.S. Open:*

My God, that's just fate, I don't know. But you could never bet against him because he could hit the ball so straight and dead on that you always knew he could knock the flagstick right out of the hole.

*Snead's good friend **Bob Goalby** was too young to have been around when Sam blew it on the seventy-second hole in Philadelphia. But forty years of being one of Snead's most trusted sounding boards gave Goalby some insights as to what happened:*

Sam hardly ever talked golf when that subject didn't come up. The one that comes to mind is the one in 1939 in

Philadelphia when he made an eight on the last hole and Byron Nelson won. He thought he needed a (birdie) four to win, and that was in the days when they didn't have scoreboards out there—you didn't have a reliable way to know what anyone else on the course was doing or what you needed to do.

But even then, why was Sam using a wood on his second shot, from the bunker, on that last hole? He gambled his ass away there, hitting the lip of the bunker with his shot in trying to reach the green in two. Even if he *had* needed a four there, he would have been better off playing his second shot back to the fairway with an iron and trying to get up and down from wedge range. That's what he should have been thinking.

I don't think he choked; I just don't think he knew exactly what he was trying to do. It might have been a lack of concentration or a lack of mental preparation. Look at Hogan; he said that in the Open he used a three-wood almost half the time where other golfers hit driver because the goal of an Open is to get the drive in the fairway.

Sam just went out there, grabbed the driver, and took a whack at it because he had a good swing and figured he had as good a chance at hitting it in the fairway as he would have with a three-wood. Every now and then it didn't hit the fairway. Sam thought he could do no wrong because he rarely did anything wrong, but you know how sports is—something always happens, such as a fumble at the wrong time. Even the best players in the world miss that little putt sometime.

I do know that Sam was a factor almost every time he played in the Open. In the play-off for the 1947 Open, which he lost to Lew Worsham, Sam must have beaten Lew by eight shots from tee to green.

At the seventeenth hole, a slight dogleg to the right, Worsham hooked his ball so far left that it went through some trees and rolled through the adjacent eighteenth fairway into some rough on the far side. He was so far off with that shot that he had a clear second shot to the green. He should have been in double-bogey territory, but instead he had a pretty makable par. From there, he hit his second shot onto the green and made par, while Sam three-putted for a bogey after having a second shot from the middle of the fairway that bounced just a bit too hard in going to the back fringe behind the green. That tied the match, and then Sam missed another short putt at the eighteenth.

***Tommy Bolt** won the 1958 U.S. Open to carve his name into golf history, right alongside his legacy of occasionally losing his temper and throwing a club. But time heals most wounds:*

I think Sam eventually got over it. To win the Open, you have to really concentrate. You have to maintain control of your emotions as well as your concentration. It's hard to win the Open. Sam and I tied for third in 1955, when Hogan and (Jack) Fleck played off.

***Bolt** got a relatively late start on the pro tour, and it took him a while to really get to know Snead:*

I didn't get to know him until after 1950 sometime, the early fifties. He had started in the thirties. I just got a late start, after having been in the service during World War II. I turned pro in 1946 and started playing in tour events in 1947. I played in eight tournaments and won money in four of them.

I played him in 1954 in the PGA, and I beat him. That was at Saint Paul. He was very popular there; I think he had won the Saint Paul Open a couple of times. The people weren't on my side too much. They were pulling for Snead, but that's the way people are—they always pull for the favorite. When I holed a putt, there wasn't much of a reaction. But when he made one, it sounded like the whole world was clapping. The morning round was really tough, and I was very fortunate to beat him one up after thirty-nine holes.

The gallery wasn't really unruly per se, but at the halfway point I threatened to quit unless they changed a little bit. I think we were even halfway through, but I told some guy in the locker room that I was thinking about not going back out to play. I told him that I was afraid that if I beat Sam Snead, they might hang me from the first tree.

Here's what ***Snead*** *once had to say about Bolt:*

After Tommy Bolt won the U.S. Open in 1958, he decided for some reason to lace into me, saying that I had an edge around long and blind greens because the fans sometimes helped keep my balls out of the rough. I'm sorry, but I think he was jealous. With that temper of his, he could never seem to get the crowds rooting for him. But in a way I don't blame him, or any of the others who took after me.[4]

Doug Ford, *another of Snead's longtime, tour-playing pals, took a different tack when it came to Snead's never winning the Open. He didn't bring the subject up in front of Snead, although he has his own conspiracy theory that somehow might involve the USGA:*

I never said anything about it to him. I always had the feeling that it was too tough a subject for him.

There was one time I was playing with him when he told me about the Open at Oakland Hills, when Hogan won (in 1951). He said that the USGA had sent off Hogan much earlier than him, and that Hogan had already finished nine holes by the time Sam started his round.

I believe that the USGA favored certain players. I remember playing at Pittsburgh (Oakmont Country Club, where Palmer lost to Nicklaus in a 1962 Open play-off). I was in the last group playing with (Cary) Middlecoff. I had been playing in the last group since Jack Fleck won the tournament in 1955, and now here it was seven years later. We got to the tenth green, and Middlecoff ran into some trouble and got hot. He left one shot in the bunker, walked out of the bunker without playing his next shot, and he said, "I'll see you later, Doug."

Suddenly, there's no one for me to play with. They had to send a scorer out to play with me the rest of the way in. After lunch they put me with Walter Burkemo's twosome playing in front of me for the last round. Before they sent us off, I went over to Joe Dey of the USGA to talk to him about this. I said, "I would like to know how come I have played in the last group for the last six years." I had had a pretty good record in the Open, finishing in the top ten for something like five of the last six years. He said, "We seed certain players and then we throw the rest in a hat." I said, "That's the dumbest thing I've ever heard." He said, "If you say another word to me, you're not going to tee off." I was ready to give it to him, but Burkemo grabbed me, and that was the end of that.

Veteran golf writer **Larry Dennis** *parlays a discussion of Snead's Open-less record into a brief discussion of who the greatest golfer was:*

Sam certainly is the greatest golfer who never won the U.S. Open, there's no question about that. I never saw Hogan or Nelson play competitively, although I saw both of them play in exhibitions. I saw Sam play competitively, but by then he was in his fifties. (Bobby) Jones was a helluva competitor, too.

A guy named Dick Mackey, who was the golf coach at Miami of Ohio and a good friend of Jack Nicklaus, did some kind of a thesis on Bobby Jones. It was virtually a stroke-by-stroke accounting of his career. You'd be surprised how many times Jones shot in the 80s, even in some of the stroke-play events. You couldn't do that today. I know how hard it is to compare eras, but was Jones as good a player as Sam Snead? No, I don't think he was.

I'm not sure where I would put Sam in an all-time ranking of great golfers. I'd put him in the top five, for sure. If you allow for a shorter period of time, I think Ben Hogan was the greatest player ever, especially for the four or five years following his 1949 auto accident. But he was a pretty good player before that, too. His putting finally got him. I remember what Sam once said in one of our panel meetings (at *Golf*

Digest) when we got to talking about putting. He said, "When Hogan was winning, from ten feet in he was the best putter there ever was." Eventually, the yips got him.

Hogan was probably the best player in history, and I would have to rate Nicklaus second for his record and longevity. Then you've got Byron Nelson, whose great play lasted eight or nine years. Then you look at Sam and realize that he lasted fifty years. He won tour events in four different decades (one of only two men ever to do that, with Raymond Floyd being the other).

There's yet another U.S. Open, in addition to the 1939 tournament at Philly and the four in which Snead was runner-up, that at least one person thinks Snead should have won. That was the 1958 U.S. Open at Southern Hills in Tulsa, Oklahoma, which Bolt won by four shots over Gary Player, and that observer is ***Freddie Haas****, whose own career overlapped much of Snead's:*

Tommy Bolt won the tournament, but I think Sam should have won it. At one dogleg hole, Tommy hit driver out into the fairway, then Sam drove it over the dogleg and into some rough. Bolt hit four-wood onto the green, about thirty feet from the pin. Sam, from the rough, then tried to hit an eight-iron to the green, but it rolled into a creek. He ended up with a six on the hole while Tommy made a four to pick up two strokes on Sam. If Sam had just hit, say, a two-iron off that tee, he still would have had just a five-iron to the green, and there's no way Tommy would have picked up two strokes there with a four-wood in his hand with Sam also hitting from the fairway with a five-iron or even a six-iron.

I don't ever remember seeing Sam lay up, like David Toms did at the last hole in winning the 2001 PGA Championship. Sam just didn't play that way. He would've gone for that green, hit it in the water, taken a stroke, hit it on the green, and taken a (double-bogey) six. That's the way he lost many of the tournaments that he lost, like in the 1939 U.S. Open in Philadelphia, when he made that eight on the last hole.

Let's move beyond the U.S. Open and take a trip overseas to the 1946 British Open. You're away, ***Johnny Bulla****:*

I threw away the British Open to Sam in 1946. We were rooming together. It was right after the war, and we didn't have very much food. So for breakfast, you could have all the fish you wanted, but you could only have one roll and one egg. Sam didn't like fish, so I gave him my roll and my egg every morning so that he would have enough to eat.

We played all our practice rounds together. In those days, everyone had to qualify for the British Open, even the defending champion. Arnold Palmer changed all that after he came along, because the boys wouldn't want to go over just to qualify, because they might then end up not even playing in the tournament. I played in it nine times and had to qualify for it every time.

I was five shots ahead of Sam going to the seventeenth hole in the first round. I was able to hit the fairway with my drive and then hit a pretty good second shot, only for it to trickle a bit off to the right onto some cobblestones that were the size of golf balls. I ended up with an eight on the hole.

On the last day, I thought I had the tournament won when I came to the seventeenth hole. I didn't want to hit my second shot over, so I hit it to the front part of the green. From there, I four-putted it. Then at eighteen, I had a five-foot putt for a birdie, and I three-putted it. I threw the tournament away. I would have won the tournament if I had finished par-par. Snead won, and that turned out to be the only time he ever won the British Open.

Snead's favorite major had to be the Masters Tournament, because it was only a day's drive from where he had grown up and he always seemed to play well at Augusta. In addition to his three victories there, he also finished second twice, to Ralph Guldahl in 1939 and to Doug Ford in 1957. When Snead won the Masters in 1949, he became the first Masters winner to be awarded what has now become the tournament's and club's trademark, a green jacket. **Bob Goalby**, *himself the winner of the 1968 Masters, takes us through Snead's play-off victory over Ben Hogan at the 1954 Masters:*

When Sam played Hogan in their play-off at the 1954 Masters, I think Hogan said only two things to Sam all day, and one them was "Good morning, Sam," on the first tee, no "Good luck" or anything like that.

One funny thing in that play-off occurred at the thirteenth (a par-five dogleg left). Ben hit his drive out to the right a little bit—not a bad drive, but he didn't get any bend on it, and it was on that little upslope on the right. He was back just far enough to make him wonder whether he should go for the green or not.

Sam hit a beautiful drive, drawing it just a little bit to the middle of the fairway. But there was a crown out there, running from the trees on the right down to the creek on the left. Sam's ball was just a little over the crown, on the downslope. In those days, in the fifties and sixties, you didn't get many good lies at Augusta, believe me. They had a one-row watering system, and when they put in the rye they had tufts of rye, and the Bermuda would kind of bend because when the wind blew it wouldn't get any water. Balls were always down a little bit in the grass. At thirteen and fifteen, it wasn't just a matter of if you were within the right distance to go for the green, it was more a matter of if you had a good enough lie to go.

So here comes Hogan, smoking his cigarette, about thirty yards behind Sam. He walks all the way up, slowly, toward where Sam was. He's going to look at Sam's lie on this little downslope before deciding what he was going to do with his own ball, because there was the matter of trying to get over the creek with the pin set in the right front of the green.

Sam knows what Hogan's coming up there for. When Hogan gets about ten feet away, Sam turns to him and says, "I'm going for it, Ben." Hogan went back and laid up with his second shot, and then Snead caught a three-iron off of that downslope and hit it to within about eight feet of the cup. Sam didn't make the eagle putt, but he made a four to go one up on Hogan, and Sam ended up winning, one up.

I must have played Augusta at least 150 times with Sam, and he would always go to that spot where his ball had been in the play-off with Hogan and point it out. You know, Hogan only beat Sam one time head to head, and that was in one of the *Shell's Wonderful World of Golf* matches down in Houston. Oh, sure, he lost medal-play events to Hogan, but I'm talking about when they had a play-off or were involved in match play somewhere.

PHOTO COURTESY OF SUZIE SNEAD

Sam tees it up at Augusta National, sometime in the eighties. Nephew J. C. Snead and Tim Simpson are the other golfers in his group, in the near background.

George Archer *came along a generation after Snead and made his own mark at Augusta by winning the 1969 Masters. By virtue of that victory, Archer earned a lifetime pass to Augusta National's social event of the year, the Tuesday night Champions Dinner, and a ringside seat to more than thirty years of Snead's most popular storytelling:*

I would see him every year at the Masters Champions Dinner. For many years the dinner would always end with Sam telling one of his jokes. And Byron Nelson didn't like any of Sam's off-color stories.

Byron was the emcee at the Masters, which is something that a lot of people don't know. He's the one who always stands up and makes a little talk, which includes some interesting stats about the tournament, such as which holes have yielded the most birdies and stuff like that. It's very nice, then dinner is closed with one of Sam's jokes.

At this point Byron and Gene Sarazen would sit there and say, "Oh, here it comes." Sam loved to tell the raunchiest stories, and they weren't funny. They were just horrible stuff, and the more horrible he could make them, the more Byron and Gene didn't like the joke. But the rest of us just loved to see all this unfold, regardless of what actually was the content of Sam's joke or story.

The first or second year after I won the Masters, I was pretty nervous about the whole thing. I remember Jimmy Demaret sitting down and looking over at Sam. "Hey, skinhead," Jimmy said, "how's your love life? Gettin' any?" And I'm sitting there thinking, Geez, *this is a whole new side of these great golf pros I've been hearing about, you know.*

I really enjoyed Sam. He loved life, and he had a good sense of humor.

Not all of Snead's Augusta memories are warm ones. While driving up to Augusta during Masters week in 1992, he ran a stop sign in Waynesboro, Georgia, and collided with another car, dislocating his left shoulder and paralyzing the driver of the other car. **Doug Ford** *was at Augusta that year and remembers the immediate aftermath:*

I can remember when he had the automobile accident in Augusta during Masters week, and he showed up at the Masters and he wasn't in good shape. His manager took Sam back to the motel and told him to go to bed, but Sam wouldn't. And he wouldn't go to the hospital, either. The manager came back and got me, saying, "He'll listen to you."

So I went and saw him and said, "C'mon, Sam, we'll go down to the emergency room and get this straightened out." It looked like he had hit himself in his head with his knee. So he said okay, and we went down to this hospital and they gave him quick service. By this time, it's five o'clock and the Champions Dinner is two hours away.

He said to me, "You'd better go back and get ready for the dinner." I left assuming that I wouldn't see him again until the next day. But he shows up at the dinner, and I said to him, "What the hell, did they give you a shot in the ass?" He said, "Oh, I feel okay." But they flew him home the next day. I tell you what: he loved the Masters. He toughed it out.

Snead's best memories of Augusta and Masters week were always about the golf. Veteran golf writer and author ***Guy Yocom*** *once wrote a* Golf Digest *article that included a summary of Snead's record at Augusta, painting a picture as he arrived in a car with Snead at the National in 1998 after a nine-hour trip up from Fort Pierce, Florida:*

We make the drive up Magnolia Lane at 2 P.M., and it is some scene as Sam gets out of the car. People freeze and stare at him. An older woman whispers to a friend, then giggles and blushes. Others call out to him. You understand better Sam's inextricable link with the Masters.

He first played there in 1937, in the depths of the Great Depression, when players wore broadcloth shirts and neckties, and corn whisky flowed at the tournament Bobby Jones called "the Augusta National Invitation." Sam finished second there in 1939 by one stroke when Ralph Guldahl shot 33 on the back nine on Sunday. It took Sam ten more years before he finally won, in 1949, donning the first green jacket ever presented. Then he won again in 1952 and once more in 1954, when he edged Ben Hogan in a play-off.

His record there is sensational. He finished second twice and was in the top ten an amazing fifteen times. He played every year until 1983, by which time he had turned in a record 146 rounds. In the context of Snead's incredible career, in which he won eighty-two times on the PGA Tour, the Masters was his most solid territory.[5]

4

Sam, Ben, and Byron: Golf's Great Triumvirate

Sam Snead, Ben Hogan, and Byron Nelson: They were three of the greatest golfers who ever lived. And they were born within eight months of each other in 1912.

Each of them still owns at least one remarkable distinction when it comes to the record books. Sam's eighty-two official tour victories are eleven more than runner-up Jack Nicklaus amassed. Nelson's eleven-victory streak in 1945, as part of his eighteen victories overall that year, has the aura and invincibility of Joe DiMaggio's fifty-six-game hitting streak. Hogan's five U.S. Open victories—by his count, anyway, including the wartime Hale America Open that had all the trappings of an official Open—are officially tabulated as four. Hogan also had that scintillating season of 1953, when he won all three majors he entered (Masters, U.S. Open, and

British Open) while winning five of the six events in which he participated.

It's a shame that there weren't more of their overlapping prime years. Nelson and Snead both were winning tournaments in their twenties, while Hogan didn't really get going until after his thirtieth birthday, which was after he had rebuilt his swing to get rid of that awful low hook. Hogan's best golf probably came after he hit forty—such as when he won his three majors in 1953, the year in which he turned forty-one. Nelson was pretty much out of the game by the time he was thirty-five, soon to be followed by Hogan's edging toward seclusion in the early fifties.

Really, the only years in which all three were hitting on all cylinders was the relatively short run of 1942 through 1946. On top of everything else, those were pretty much the war years, which interrupted tournament play and saw a number of golfers, Hogan and Snead included, forced to put the tour on a back burner at times while serving some time in the military.

The best golf rivalries are usually born out of down-to-the-wire battles in major events. Surprisingly, these three were involved in one-two finishes in majors only three times: when Hogan won the 1942 Masters and Nelson finished second; 1953, when Hogan won the U.S. Open over Snead; and 1954, when Snead beat Hogan in a Masters play-off.

No matter, this trio deserves mention as the sport's best-ever triumvirate, edging out the second-best, in part because there was always some disagreement over who deserved to be No. 3 behind Jack Nicklaus and Arnold Palmer. A case could be made for Gary Player; others argue for Billy Casper. You could even include Lee Trevino in the mix, although by the time Trevino was winning majors and pushing Nicklaus to the limit, Palmer was on the outs, Arnie's last major having come at the 1964 Masters, a full four years before Trevino won his first, the 1968 U.S. Open.

The special essence of the Snead-Hogan-Nelson triumvirate goes far beyond their on-course rivalry and places in the record books. Each in his own way made, or has made, an enduring impact on the game. For Snead, it was his being able to compete against the best in the world into his sixties and even into his seventies when matched against players a generation younger on what is now the Champions Tour. For Nelson, it has been his hands-on association with the official PGA Tour event named after him, the only golfer accorded such an honor. For Hogan, it was the Hogan Company, which he helped start fifty years ago, and in part his Howard Hughesian seclusion for most of the last thirty years of his life.

Picking one of these three as the best of the lot would be a mistake, even in a book that zeroes in on Snead. Still, the differences in opinions on the subject are intriguing.

Chi Chi Rodriguez, *veteran golfer familiar with all three:*

They're like wallpaper: everybody's different. But they were all great guys, and they just might have been the three greatest players who ever lived.

Bob Toski:

They comprised the greatest triumvirate ever. It would be like putting Citation, Whirlaway, and whatever horse you want next to each other. That's it. No one has ever hit the flagstick more times than Byron (Nelson) did. And no one will ever win eleven tournaments in a row like he did.

Doug Ford:

I think Snead's the greatest player who ever lived. But then you talk to Snead, and he'll tell you how great Byron Nelson was. And I thought Hogan might have been a better player than Nelson, but then again, I only saw Nelson after he had retired from tournament golf. I had played with Hogan when he was at his best. But Snead still, to me, could hit the best shots, and he could hit all the shots.[1]

Okay, let's dig a little deeper into this and turn to ***Freddie Haas****, who played the tour for a number of years alongside the big three:*

Sam was stronger than either Nelson or Hogan. He was stronger than anybody out there, except maybe Jimmy Thomson.

The driving contests we had out there would really develop into something. We would go to the driving range, and whoever hit the ball the farthest would win either a hundred or two hundred dollars. Most of the time it was only a hundred.

It was quite a match between Jimmy Thomson, who was very strong and had a very good swing, and Sam Snead. But Sam could not get the ball up into the air quite as much as Jimmy could, or even as much as Nelson or Hogan could, for that matter. Sam's lower ball would run, sure, but a lot of the times his ball would run into the rough or into the water.

I think Sam would have been better off if he had used a more lofted wood such as a three- or four-wood to get the ball up into the air, because he hit it so straight he could have placed it better. But he hit his driver low and when it was dry, it would often roll too far into some place not too favorable. The longer your ball is on the ground, the more trouble it can get into.

Johnny Bulla *is in the same boat as Haas in being qualified from personal experience to compare and contrast the three. It should be pointed out, however, that Bulla knew Snead better than he did the other two because he and Snead often traveled together on tour for a number of years:*

Hogan wasn't a great player in the beginning. He didn't even win a tournament until he was almost thirty years old. He was very inconsistent. He was the hardest worker out there, but he wasn't that consistent because he always swayed on his hip when swinging. It wasn't until the fifties that he played his best golf.

Nelson could do it all. He could hit it straight and he could putt the ball.

Snead wasn't just the most natural golfer of the three, he was the most natural player ever to play the game.

They got along very strangely. They didn't really socialize at all, even though they were very cordial with each other on the golf course. Ben didn't get along with Byron because Byron beat him too many times. Hogan was really jealous of Byron. I remember one time when they tied at the Texas

Open in San Antonio. Before the play-off, they had both guys on the radio. Ben said to Byron, "I hope you lose tomorrow because you never practice." But Byron beat him.

I can't remember Ben ever beating Byron head to head in a tournament, and then Byron quit competing at a pretty young age. You've got to remember, however, that Byron won a lot while Snead and Hogan were both in the service during World War II. But he still played great golf.

Freddie Haas *turned pro in 1946, which was Nelson's last full year on tour, which is why he knew Snead and Hogan a bit better:*

They were all different. Hogan kept pretty much to himself. (Cary) Middlecoff and I played several exhibitions in Memphis with (Jimmy) Demaret and Hogan. After we got through playing, Hogan was wonderful, a clever fellow with a nice sense of humor, and was fine . . . until we got on the golf course.

There was one hole there where I holed about a thirty- or forty-foot putt, and I was carrying on a little bit about that. Hogan, meanwhile, had a putt from about six feet to tie the hole, and he stays there behind the ball and makes no attempt to hit it. It dawned on me that I hadn't yet picked my ball up out of the hole, and he says to me, "Will you . . . please . . . complete . . . your play?"

That night at dinner I said to him, "Ben, I want to apologize. I shouldn't have carried on like that, but I was excited about making that long a putt. We won't carry on like that anymore."

"That's okay," he said, "I know why you did it." I was forgiven, I hope.

Hogan was a strong guy, but he wasn't a big man, and he could not hit the ball as far as Sam Snead could. I also thought Snead was a better putter than Hogan, and that that gave him an advantage of about half a stroke a round over Ben.

As far as Nelson is concerned, when he was on, it was a toss-up. But overall, I think Snead was about a quarter-shot a round better than Byron. It seems whenever Hogan and Snead had a play-off, Sam would beat him by a stroke. Hogan got even with Sam, though, one time on *Shell's Wonderful World of Golf*, when he played a superb round, not missing a shot, and really put it on Sam.

I thought Sam Snead was the best player, but he did not manage the golf course. And he didn't win the majors that he should have.

Haas *continues his evaluation of the big three by bringing Tiger Woods into the equation:*

It looks like Tiger Woods is going to have the best record in golf by the time he gets through, which, potentially, would make him the best player of all time. But I see him winning all of these tournaments, and I look at the supporting cast that he's playing against, and I say to myself, *I'd like to see Snead, Nelson, and Hogan in that mix.*

I've always tried to figure out in my head what would happen if Tiger Woods, Sam Snead, Ben Hogan, and Byron Nelson were all within one stroke of each other going into the final round of a major. What would happen? You can bet your bottom dollar that one of those other three guys is going to shoot a pretty low score. I see some of the tournaments that Tiger has won, and I don't see anybody shooting a low score against him.

The question comes up, What is the best supporting cast to Tiger? Would it be Phil Mickelson, Ernie Els, and Vijay Singh, or somebody else like that? Which group of players would you bet on to beat Tiger—those three or someone out of the group of Snead, Hogan, and Nelson? I think I'd bet on the latter group. Don't forget that the equipment those guys played with fifty years ago doesn't at all compare to what is being routinely used today.

The greatest? Again, **Doug Ford** *weighs in with a vote for his pal Snead:*

I think Sam was the greatest golfer who ever lived. You can talk about (Ben) Hogan or whomever. Let me say this, if you got him talking he would tell you what he thought, and he believed that (Byron) Nelson was a better player than Hogan.

Ben Crenshaw *probably knows more about the history of golf and its great players than anyone else who has played the PGA Tour since 1980. Keep in mind that Crenshaw is good friends with Nelson and practically idolized Hogan:*

I never saw Byron Nelson play, and I've only seen Ben Hogan hit balls. But I've played a lot with Sam, and he plays the game the way it's supposed to be played—the way you dream about playing just once in your life.[2]

***Snead** made no secret of his resentment over the fact that Hogan was voted the tour's player of the year in 1950. That was the year in which Hogan made a remarkable comeback from his near-fatal car crash of 1949 and won the U.S. Open, his only victory that year against Snead's eleven. Here's what Sam once had to say about Hogan:*

Ben Hogan may have been the greatest golfer of my generation. Nobody was as dedicated to golf as he was. He threw everything else aside. We might have been buddies in another life, but it just so happened that we both came into our prime at exactly the same time. It was fated that we'd become the two great rivals of American golf.[3]

*Okay, **Snead**, enough of the Hogan platitudes. Tell us how you really felt about Hogan's winning Golfer of the Year honors in 1950:*

Of course, 1950 was Ben's comeback year after his near-fatal car accident. It was called "the greatest comeback in sports history," and I won't argue with that. Heck, they could have given him a six-foot trophy as the best comeback kid, but he just wasn't the best player that year. After that, I said, "The hell with it," and cut back on my playing significantly. . . . It hurts even now.[4]

***Snead** wasn't enamored of Hogan's smoking habit, either:*

Ben was a hard player to read because he kept his emotions to himself. But once he started to get the yippies, you could tell right away he was struggling. He'd smoke a whole cigarette before he could bring himself to try and putt.[5]

As nephew **J. C. Snead** *suggests, the highlight of Sam's career might have been his 1954 Masters victory over Hogan. J. C. knows this because of how well his uncle could recall almost every sight and sound from their play-off round:*

Sam would get so upset when people would talk about how Hogan had played so well in the play-off at the 1954 Masters. Sam would go through the whole round and tell you about every shot and where he hit it. I don't think he missed a green, although he would call hitting a par-five in two as being one under regulation.

Sam Snead *shifts the discussion to Byron Nelson:*

Byron is a very gentle man, but he has a streak of steel. He was a very tough competitor but very fair. When he was playing well, he kept pretty much to himself, but when he got off his game, he became more talkative.[6]

Tour veteran **John Mahaffey** *is one of the few golfers under the age of sixty who can claim close ties with at least two of the three golfers—Snead and Hogan. Mahaffey played Hogan's clubs for a number of years, and anyone who repped the Hogan Company was in pretty tight with the old man. But Mahaffey also got to know Snead well, and today Mahaffey is one of J. C. Snead's best friends on the Champions Tour:*

AP/WIDE WORLD PHOTO

Even at age sixty-six, Snead looks loose and limber during a round at the Saint Clair Country Club in Belleville, Illinois.

I knew Hogan better because I was with his company, and I spent more time with Ben than I did with Sam.

Hogan wanted to get as close to perfection as he could possibly get, and he probably was that way in how he approached the game. It was very much a business to him. Sam really loved to play, and it was a game to him. Their approach was different, but it's hard to say whether one really enjoyed the game more than the other. I didn't know Byron that well and didn't play him with as much.

Sam could have done about any kind of athletic endeavor. From a young age he had a golf swing that he just honed over the years, where Hogan had to go out and build one. I don't think Sam was as concerned with all the components of the golf swing. Not that he didn't know them and didn't know what to do whenever he might have gotten off track, but he had that natural ability, a gift that few others have. Sam might have had to make minor adjustments, such as with his alignment, but nothing much more than that. Nelson had a lot of that, too. Hogan had to make a lot of major changes before he started winning as a pro, and Nelson was somewhere in the middle of those two.

Sam came from a background where he spent a lot of time in the outdoors hunting and fishing, and golf just kind of fit in with all that. Sam just loved to play golf. And that swing—comparing my swing to his would be like comparing hamburger to filet. I've got a pretty simple golf swing, and it's one that J. C. has helped me on some, with some very simple things.

I never really knew Sam, but when I got the chance to be up there with him and to visit with him, including having dinner with him one night—he and J. C. and some of the family—I found that he was a really nice man. He didn't have to show me around the house and show me all these neat things that meant so much to him, but he did.

Bob Toski *saw the different sides of Sam Snead, the one as a generous provider who didn't want notoriety for his charity work, and the other as a true Hogan rival:*

One thing that a lot of people don't know about Sam is that he helped a lot of kids on tour who had really been struggling. He gave money to young players who might otherwise have never made it.

I remember one time after watching Hogan practice, I was out there practicing myself, trying to emulate some of Hogan's moves. I wasn't afraid to try something new, and I had been watching Hogan flatten out his swing, and he also had a lot of lateral motion in the downswing. He had a lot of speed. He complemented the upper body's speed and the angle set by the hands and wrists by a lower drive to keep that angle. So I'm out there trying to hit balls using some of Hogan's moves.

All this time, Sam is off to the side watching me. He finally walks over and says, "Mouse, what in the hell are you doing?" I said, "Sam, I'm working on my swing." He said, "Well, you don't look like you're swinging the way you should be swinging."

Let me tell you how perceptive Sam was. I told him, "I've been watching Ben practice, and I'm trying to incorporate a few of those moves in my swing." Of course, Hogan would never say anything to you; he would just let you watch him practice. Sam says, "You know, Mouse, Bob Toski has got a beautiful golf swing. You don't need to copy Hogan's swing to be a successful player. You've got a swing that Bob Toski ought to play golf with. You go back and swing like Bob Toski. Now put those hands back up where you had them. Get that thing up there where you can get some speed."

Boy, when Sam told me that, I said to myself, *You had better do it!* So I hit a few more shots, and he said a few more things, telling me that I was back to swinging the way I should be. That's the kind of lesson that Sam Snead gave you.

5

Sam the Man

In some respects, Sam Snead was a man's man. A certain kind of man's man. He was a bit rough around the edges, with a fondness for coloring his jokes with a lot of blue language. He also had a passion for any golf game accompanied by a ten-dollar nassau and a hankering for showing off when the right moments presented themselves. Stick a hickory-shafted brassie in his hands, toss a ball onto the hard deck at his feet, and tell him he can't hit a high draw around and over that eighty-foot elm 180 yards down the fairway, and that would light his competitive fire.

Those who didn't really know Snead would write him off as a country bumpkin, as just another a hillbilly who would have felt right at home with Jed, Granny, Jethro, and Elly May. Not so. Snead had a knack for being able to fit in with about anybody from any slice of life, especially if they knew how to play golf, and play it fairly well.

When asked or prodded, Sam could play to the stereotype: he once posed for a publicity shot dressed like a barefoot Li'l Abner in cutoff suspendered pants and a beat-up straw hat. Just to have some fun with promoters, following a photo appearance of him in *The New York Times*, Snead wondered aloud how the paper had obtained the photo because he "had never been to New York." Grin and bear it.

In eulogizing Snead, former amateur champion Bill Campbell said, "Sam was a physical phenomenon with boundless energy and stamina. He had the eye of an eagle, the grace of a leopard, and the strength and heart of a lion." There is so much to Snead, whose fluid, graceful swing disguised the power that lurked beneath. He could play the banjo and carry a tune pretty well, and he had a way with animals, including the fish in his backyard pond that would let Sam pick it up and pet it. He also wrote a bunch of books about golf, such as *Pigeons, Marks, and Hustlers*—a guide to betting on golf that he co-authored with Jerry Tarde.

If he hadn't been a pro golfer, Snead might just as easily have been a running back in football or some sort of track star. Or a tailor; his mom taught him how to sew. In fact, Sam was as adept at making any necessary repairs in his attire while on the road as any seamstress could have been. Above all else, though, he loved golf. After marrying Audry Karnes in 1940, they set out on a honeymoon that took them to Niagara Falls en route to the Canadian Open, which he won that year.

***Chi Chi Rodriguez** came along on tour about twenty-five years after Snead had started, but Snead was still around on tour well into Rodriguez's own career:*

Sam Snead might have been the greatest athlete of all time. He was kind of a hillbilly, and you can't put a tuxedo on a hillbilly. He was just what he was—the best golfer in the world and a nice person. It's a shame that they have never named a trophy after Sam Snead or named anything for him at Augusta, like a bridge or something, even though he won the Masters three times. He won 106 tournaments, and they give him credit for eighty-two. They have taken everything away from him. One year he won eleven tournaments, Hogan won one, and they gave Hogan the player of the year. That's awful.

They also used to give Sam bad starting times because they didn't want him to win. In the old days, you know, golf was a fix. They used to fix the pairings, they used to fix the starting times, and they used to fix the pin placements in such a way that certain guys would have a better chance to win. Sam never got the best shake on anything; he just won because he was better.

I talked to him a lot, and Sam was bitter. But he could take it. Sam was the best. God bless him.

Lee Trevino:

Sam was a great athlete. He didn't drink until he was in his sixties, and he didn't smoke, even when he advertised cigarettes.

Snead *was a borderline health nut, avoiding popular vices long before it became fashionable to eat well and live a healthy lifestyle. He explained how he was able to live a long, mostly healthy life while competing against men a generation or two younger:*

Living in moderation has paid full dividends for me over the years. I'm sure of that. I've not only stayed away from the hooch, but I've also refrained from smoking, at least since way back when I was starting high school. I did take a couple of puffs many years ago when I was doing some cigarette commercials, but my mouth tasted terrible for a week.

Maybe I won't convince you to give up drinking and smoking in order to play better golf longer—that's your business—but I do feel obligated to point out that both can affect your skills. Alcohol, like caffeine, can make you jumpy under pressure, and older people especially don't need something extra to stimulate those frayed nerves.[1]

***Dave Stockton**, although almost thirty years younger than Snead, knew how tough a competitor Sam could be even in his sixties. When Stockton won the Glen Campbell Los Angeles Open at Riviera in 1974, sixty-one-year-old Sam Snead tied for second, two shots back:*

Sam Snead was kind of our Mickey Mantle in terms of the athletic things that he was able to do. He had a marvelous swing and he was competitive (on the PGA Tour), even into his sixties.

Sam was like Mantle in that he could have played any sport he wanted to because he had the physical tools to do so. Plus, he had so much flexibility. As a lot of us get older, we stiffen up, and he was able to reverse, or at least delay, that process. He was absolutely incredible.

He was tough to play with because he was such a competitor, from the old school. He would try to influence you.

I had to be very careful to play my own game. Still, you loved watching him hit the ball because he had such great rhythm.

Peter Thomson, who won the British Open five times:

Like the classic plays and symphonies, Sam Snead doesn't belong to just one generation. His mark will be left on golf for eternity.[2]

George Archer:

When you think of those guys from his generation, like Hogan, Demaret, and Nelson, you could see where each one had such a different personality. The sad thing today isn't that the young guys don't have any personality—they do. It's just that they have to be so careful about it. Some of the things that guys used to get away with years ago, guys today would just get nailed to the cross for.

You look at Babe Ruth and hear all the stories about him and the women, and how he would leave the bench in the middle of a game to go get a couple of hotdogs. Sports has changed, and that includes golf. With Tiger Woods doing so much exercise combined with his great success, he has really raised the bar so high that everybody else is trying to be him, and to do that, they realize they have to exercise like crazy. This kid has done a fabulous job of handling his life, and so far he hasn't come out of his skin yet, like other guys have done. Golf is his business, and he's very selective about what he does and doesn't do.

Warm and fuzzy were not Sam Snead trademarks, as his nephew **J. C. Snead** *found out at an early age:*

Every once in a while, while I was in high school, Sam would come to a football game or a basketball game.

They had a couple of little tournaments up at The Homestead, including a fall festival, where I would go out there and watch him. I never would go up to him—I was always kind of shy, and I would stay back in the background. He'd see me. He'd cut his eyes out around from under that hat, and he would see me and not say a word.

When he said something, it always hurt my feelings. It was like, "Boy, what the hell are you doing out here? Why aren't you caddying and making some money?" Always something surly. It was never, "Hey, good to see you. How's your dad?" or "How's your mom?" I'd go along for six, seven, or eight holes, and he would say something like that to me, and I would just get the hell out of there because my feelings were hurt. I would just kind of crawl away, like a stupid little dog or something. That's the way it was for a long time.

After I got onto the golf tour (in 1968, at age twenty-eight), he was fantastic to me. He knew I was really serious about making a go of it, and from then on he would do whatever he could to help me out. I stayed at his apartment. He took me out to dinner, never letting me pick up the tab. I was married at the time, and he was good to my wife. He got me a set of clubs after insinuating for a while that my clubs weren't any good, although I never took the hint. Finally, one day he just said, "Boy, why don't you just get rid of those damn things? They're too short. Here, let me show you." Well, he showed me, and after that I knew what he was talking about, and I got rid of those golf clubs. And he gave me a set of his.

I would play every practice round with him before tournaments, playing with guys like Bob Goalby, Doug Ford, and Jerry Barber. Every chance I got, I played with Sam. He was great, and we had a great relationship. We became very close, and it was like he was another father to me.

J. C. Snead *goes on to explain how the ice between he and Sam finally began to melt after J. C. was well into his twenties forging his own career in pro golf:*

When Sam would come home, my dad and I would go over to see him. They would sit there and B.S. But he never talked about golf, very seldom. He was always talking about something like hunting or fishing. I never heard him say much about other golf pros, including criticizing other players.

When I was about fifteen or sixteen, he would sometimes take me fishing with him. He also took me hunting a couple of times, and that was a big thrill. He gave me a fishing rod and once let me wear his fishing boots, although I tore a hole in one of them. It seems like every time I did something with him, something would break or something like that. There was one time when I was shagging balls for him at home, and I was catching them in a bag and broke a zipper on it. Stuff just always seemed to happen.

The first time I played golf with him was actually in 1968 at Boca Raton. I stayed with his older brother, my Uncle Homer, and I played with him three, four, or five times a week. We played for a little money, and I was always his partner. The first time I played with him I was probably as nervous as I've ever been playing golf. Oh, yeah, I was scared to death.

He was really good to me after he realized that I was serious about playing and that I was going to try and make a go of it on the tour. I didn't even start playing golf seriously until I was twenty-four. This wasn't one of those classic stories where the great-playing uncle took aside his young nephew at an early age and put a golf club in his hands.

I used to caddie as a kid when I was up at Hot Springs at The Homestead, but they wouldn't let kids on the golf course back then—they would run you off. They had a little old "goat course," they called it, and I would get a club or two and go play, although I couldn't play a lick. I always played baseball. I didn't have time to play golf. I started playing semipro baseball when I was fifteen, and I always had a job in the summer, so I never really had time to play golf.

I played pro baseball for three and a half years, and would come home around Labor Day after the baseball season was over. I would still have several weeks before I had to go back to college, and I didn't have anything to do in that time. So I started caddying a little bit, and then late in the day as evening came in I would go out on the golf course and play.

All of a sudden my Uncle Pete gave me a lesson and showed me how to use my hands, and that's how I got rid of that big banana slice I had played with every time I picked up a club. And just like that, golf became fun for me. In baseball you might hit the ball four hundred feet and in golf you hit the ball three hundred fifty yards, and that's a real eye-opener. I just wanted to see how far it would go. I didn't care where it went when I first started out. I could fly it three hundred yards, no problem, except I didn't know where the hell it was going. Half the time it went dead right.

I had three uncles who were golf pros, and I started thinking that if I didn't make it in baseball, I could always just be a golf pro, because I liked sports and I liked being outdoors, although I had no intent of going on the golf tour. I never even thought about that. I went to work in White Plains, New York, at a country club for a friend of mine. I worked in a golf shop, cleaning up clubs and picking up range balls. Then the next year I started teaching, and I spent four summers there.

I had been up there two summers, and Sam was doing an exhibition with four or five other pros at a club not too far away from where I was working. The guy I worked for used to work for Sam, so he took me over there and asked Sam to take a look at me. By this time, I was about twenty-five. But when we got over there, Sam didn't even have time for me. To him, I was just another kid trying to get something off of him or something like that. That was just kind of his attitude, and it ticked me off. I didn't want anything to do with him after that for a long time. I said in my mind, *Screw 'im.*

I stayed up there and worked for another couple of summers, before I went to Puerto Rico to work one winter. While I was there, I played with Chi Chi (Rodriguez), and he quit after six holes because I was outdriving him by about eighty yards. He didn't want any more of that, although he jokes about it now, that I was making him look bad in front of his fans. But I was a horrendous wedge player and couldn't putt very well.

The members at that club in White Plains wanted me to try out for the tour. So I tried to qualify twice, even though I had never played in a tournament. I had a perfect record as an amateur: zero. I got my A card for the PGA Tour, and with some members back at the club sponsoring me, I went out on tour.

That's when I went down and stayed with my other uncle, Homer, and that's when Sam realized that I was really serious about trying to play golf. He'd take me up to Boca and partner with me, and we would make twenty-five to thirty bucks a day, which back then wasn't all that bad. He was a helluva partner, and I could just freewheel everything. If I missed a shot, that was okay; and if I hit a good one, that was great.

George Archer:

Sam could be rough. I saw that at different times.

One time Sam was up at Laurel Valley. This is a classic. They had a nice little hamburger and milkshake place there, sort of like a Dairy Queen, but this was before the chains. Mom and pop owned this little spot, and everyone up there in that neck of the woods knew this was the place to go to get a burger.

One day my wife and I were going in there to get our hamburger and milkshake. And we spotted Sam with a lady friend who had been a college professor at Stanford University. Very nice lady. He's leaving, and he gets into this big Lincoln that he had, and there was this telephone pole there. He had his milkshake and his hamburger in his hand and on his lap, and he backs right up into the telephone pole. The milkshake and hamburger go all over him because he's trying to eat at the same time he's backing up.

The two of them jump out of the car, and she's teed off, to say the least. I mean, there's only one telephone pole in this whole parking lot, and he found it. It dented the bumper, and it was one of those deals where you couldn't just go and claim that someone had run into your car. You could tell by the indentation that he had hit a pole. I kidded Sam about that for a long time. "Hey, Sam, have you had any good burgers lately." "Awww, shut up, Archer." He was a guy who could take a kidding, and he loved to give a kidding.

Gary Player *once lost a footrace to Snead, more than twenty years senior to him, and beating Snead at golf often proved to be just as difficult. Player knew enough about Snead's background to know that Sam's longevity and superior athleticism were family traits:*

He had the genes, no question about it. That Snead family all had incredible genes: All were big and strong, and they lived a long time.

When I won the PGA in 1972 at Oakland Hills, Sam was right in there (finishing third). He was a heckuva competitor. It would have been interesting to see how well, while in his prime, he could have played against these young guys of today with all this great equipment and all this prize money and all these private jets and all these entourages. Of everyone now out there on tour, the only one who could have beaten him was Tiger Woods, and I'm not sure Tiger could have. It would have been a very good match.

Johnny Bulla, *Snead's frequent traveling companion for about six years on the early tour, came to appreciate the side of Snead that demonstrated loyalty to friends:*

Let me tell you what kind of a guy Sam was. He stood up for his principles and for his friends.

He had the best contract of any pro in the business. One time we were getting ready to play in the Chicago Open. That Monday, Sam's manufacturing rep asked to see him at the factory, and I was waiting for him out in the car. After some time, Sam came walking back out to the car, and his face was beet red. I figured he had gotten fired from his contract or something. But that wasn't the case.

It turns out that the guy had told Sam that I was bad for the game and that Sam shouldn't be hanging around with me anymore. Sam told me that he told the guy, "You can tell me what clubs to play, what ball to play, and where to go, but you never tell me who I have to keep company with." The thing with me is that I was using a line of equipment different from what the other pros were using, and I was seen by some as a bad influence.

Sam would always tell you exactly what he thought and he was loyal, and that was a good trait. But I tell you one thing: If you ever made him mad, you had better be sure to get out of the way. I made him mad once, and that was on an occasion when we were playing hearts for dimes. He beat me every time. I just couldn't beat him. So I quit.

About a week later, I see him seated with a checkerboard. "Do you play checkers?" he asked me. I said, "I don't know. Why?" So he said, "Let's play some checkers."

Well, truth be told, I was the best checkers player on tour. I beat him a couple of times and let him beat me a couple of times. One day soon after that, he asked me, "Boo-boo, how good are you, really?" I said, "Sam, if you play me again, you'll never beat me." And so I showed him. He said afterward, "You trapped me. You took my money." Oh, he was so mad, but I told him that I had to do something to get back at him for beating me so badly at hearts. He said, "Hah, this is still dishonest." He was really mad.

So he went and got a book on checkers and studied it and studied it. He was determined that I wasn't going to beat him at anything. Sometime later we were at a tournament site, and he challenged me again to play some checkers. I met him down in the lobby of the hotel we were staying in, and I beat him three straight games. He never did beat me. It was only later that I told him that I had learned to play checkers from a guy who had won state championships in three states.

In his classic book Uphill Is Easier, *former CBS-TV sports commentator* ***John Derr*** *tells about how he came to know Snead as someone who wasn't all that he was purported to be, thankfully:*

Sam Snead caused me my biggest problem in my reportorial career—in print and on the air.

When I became a professional reporter, my first editor impressed upon me the fact that I had forfeited my right to be a fan. Thereafter my job would be to report who won and how. Nothing more.

Where Snead was involved with all this was difficult because I was undeniably a Snead fan. I loved to watch him swing the club. . . .

Throughout his career Snead stirred up negative emotions in some who spoke unkindly of him. It never bothered Snead, but it did me. Most of their disenchantment was from second-hand rumors, misunderstandings to humor their own egos.

I've heard people tell how rude he was when pie-eyed in a bar in Phoenix. I knew Sam didn't drink, so that couldn't have been. Maybe a beer or wine at dinner, but he was not a drinker.[3]

Derr, *with another of his favorite Snead stories, from* Uphill Is Easier*:*

One year at the Tam O'Shanter tournament in Chicago, Snead shot 68 the first round and followed with a 66. I sat in the press room for his bubbling interview and then together we walked out toward the parking lot.

As we walked briskly, side by side, at about the same moment we both saw a dollar bill in the path ahead. Neither said a word, but our pace quickened. When within a few feet, I dashed forward and planted my shoe on the bill.

Snead thought he could reach it quicker by grabbing for it, and we got there simultaneously, him holding one end in his hand. The rest of it was under my foot.

"Lift up your foot," he said. "I saw it first."

"Yes, but I reached it first."

"Take your shoe off, or I'll tear it (the dollar bill) in two."

No deal.

Sam reached in his pocket and gave me two quarters for my half. We each were fifty cents richer, but that fifty cents represented his entire winnings for the week. In lunging to grab it first, he had put his entire weight on his wrist and sprained it. Overnight it became swollen and sore.

When I arrived in the press room at Tam O'Shanter the next day, there was a note on the bulletin board: "Snead has withdrawn. Re-injured sore wrist."[4]

One of the casualties of Snead's love for golf and a life chasing paychecks on the tour was a decent family life back home in Virginia. **Jack Snead**, *the older of Sam and Audry's two boys, remembers:*

When I was a kid, Dad was gone forty weeks of the year. He seemed to be gone in eight-week clips. I missed him so much. My favorite time was Thanksgiving, because the whole family would gather, and we got to spend the whole weekend together. My mom would make big lunches for the men, and they'd take off hunting. They let me go with them. There hasn't been an occasion since I enjoyed more.

The stories they told! We had an uncle who lived during the Civil War they called Big John Snead, who stood seven-foot-nine, weighed 350 pounds, and wore a size twenty-seven shoe. It's true; I looked him up in the hall of records in Warm Springs. In those days they had fence-building parties, where the men would gather and fence a neighbor's pasture. The women would cook and sew, while the men cut these huge chestnut trees into eleven-foot rails. The wood was green and heavy; a stout man could lift four or five of them. Well, one day somebody asked where Big John was, and here he came over a hill, carrying six over each shoulder. We Sneads have always been plain people, but we were unusual.[5]

Jack Snead's *admiration for his dad was evident, as when he talked about Sam's physical prowess:*

For years Dad carried around an exercise contraption made of handles and springs, the kind bodybuilders would pull across their chests in magazine advertisements. As it got old and rusty, it got harder to stretch. Men would take that thing and couldn't stretch it at all. Hell, they couldn't stretch it using their legs. Dad would just smile and pull that thing back and forth like an accordion.[6]

***Freddie Haas**, one of Sam's tour peers, also marveled at Snead's athletic ability:*

Sam was stronger than everybody else, and more limber, too. He was a physical marvel, really, and he was able to do an awful lot of things, even into his eighties. It wasn't until the last four or five years of his life that his swing became short.

He had the best forward press on his swing for any golfer I've ever seen. He kind of worked it to a point where the more he did it, the farther you knew he was going to hit it. It was the most beautiful forward press to see, just before his backswing: You could see it just building up his strength. It was just magnificent.

***Byron Nelson**:*

Sam was like a cat. His coordination and his movements were so athletic, so different from most players'. When I would be playing with Sam, he would surprise you with the things he could do. We would walk off a tee, and if there was a bench there he'd hop over it just like a rabbit.[7]

*Count **Tommy Bolt** among the hundreds, perhaps thousands, who witnessed Snead's kicking the top of a doorjamb or low* *ceiling on occasion, displaying a leg kick that would have been the envy of the June Taylor Dancers. Sometimes, though, things didn't always go so well:*

I remember one time at the J. C. Penney Classic when he came walking into the locker room with all these younger guys around and we told him to kick the ceiling. He stops and—*wham!*—he kicks the ceiling but sprains his big toe a little bit. He didn't mean to kick so high. But he was still able to play.

***Bob Goalby**:*

Sam could kick the top of that door until he was eighty-five, and he could do one-armed pushups until you got tired of watching. He could get the ball out of the bottom of the cup without bending his knees. I saw him one time punting a football behind the hotel, and almost every one of them was a spiral of at least forty yards. He could beat you with a fishing rod, beat you shooting pool, beat you pitching pennies. . . . No matter what you did with him, he was better than you were.

Sam was a phenomenal athlete. One year we were at the Masters playing a practice round, and he was pretty old at this time. We get down to number two, and the (gallery) ropes were about a foot and a half or two feet off the ground. When we walked off the green, he was feeling pretty spry, and instead of walking through where they had put the opening in the ropes, he walked over to where the ropes were up, jumped over the rope, clicked his heels midway, and then landed on the other side without missing a beat. I guarantee you that anybody else would have fallen and hit the damn ropes. I wouldn't even think of trying, and I was seventeen years younger than him.

I don't believe there've ever been many athletes with his agility, his double-jointedness, or his sense of rhythm and timing. That's why he could always strike a golf ball so well, even when he was very young or quite old.

Goalby *recalls how Snead's occasional demonstrations of extraordinary physical fitness weren't limited just to high kicks but to finishing kicks as well:*

Down at Pensacola one year, Gary Player was talking about how he had once been a track star in his high school days. Snead was listening to all this and finally said, "Hell, I'm twenty years older than you, and I can beat your ass any day."

So the bets were made in the locker room, and this was on a day when the round had been rained out. Everyone went out to the first tee at Pensacola Country Club and measured off a hundred yards down the fairway, with a rope at the end marking the finish line.

Everyone thought Gary was going to kill Sam. They lined up at the start line, the starter got them started, and off they went. At around sixty yards, Gary was about ten yards behind Sam and came up lame. Sam was smoking him—he was going to beat him by twenty yards! To this day, I don't think Gary was really a track star, even though he might have run some track.

George Archer*:*

Sam Snead at sixty-something was ridiculous. There were guys in their thirties who couldn't do things that Sam could do. He worked out, and he would sometimes ask you to feel his belly, and it would be as hard as this table I'm sitting next to. He was very solid. Even though he didn't talk much about exercising, he did it. He didn't have a physique like he did for as long as he did unless he did things like that to stay in such great shape.

I heard stories of how he would walk into Greenbrier early in the morning and do thirty minutes of exercise. That's how he kept the flexibility and shape that he was in. Otherwise, he never would have played as well as he did for such a long time. He worked at it, but he also was gifted with that great flexibility. To be able to stand on one leg and raise the other leg right up to your nose is amazing, and I saw him doing that into his seventies. Instead of shaking my hand when he saw me, he would just say, "Put it up there," and I knew what he meant. I'd hold up a hand and he would put his foot up and just lightly touch it. "Still got it, don't I?" Then he'd laugh and walk off.

Snead not only had power and a burst of speed, but his endurance was legendary, mostly in terms of his longevity as a competitive golfer. **Johnny Bulla***:*

Longevity comes from lifestyle. Walking is one of the best exercises there is, and that's one of the reasons Arnold Palmer has stood up so well for so long—it's because he has walked so much.

The problem with some guys, and it's as much a problem today as it was when I was playing, is that they drink too much. The few that really take care of themselves are the ones that are winning, and Tiger takes great care of himself. Sam did, too. Somebody asked me the other day how old I was, and I said, "I'm just a few days short of ninety, and I'll be middle-aged before I know it." I'm eighty-eight and my eyes are in perfect shape.

Sam didn't drink at all until after he couldn't play golf anymore. Although he didn't do much exercise away from the golf course, he didn't have to. He played golf every day, and that kept him in shape. He was one of those guys who would wake up every morning with the attitude that he couldn't wait to get up and play again. He had that discipline and desire. And it was a desire to beat somebody. He just loved competition.

The first thing that comes to mind when picturing current Champions Tour star ***Fuzzy Zoeller*** *isn't necessarily physical fitness. Zoeller without a cigarette in hand is like Dean Martin without a martini. But being the gregarious guy that he is, Zoeller only naturally befriended the fit-as-a-fiddle Snead, and he did so at an early age:*

I first met him when I was fourteen years old. I met him at a golf course in Hollywood, Florida. It was kind of neat; my uncle told me to come out there, and I came over as a runny-nosed kid. He was playing golf with Sam. I didn't even take my clubs out there. I just went out there to meet the legend, and he was definitely a legend.

I loved him. He was always good to me. Every time I saw Sam, we always had something to talk about, including war stories about my uncle. He was a good entertainer, but for men only. Not for women. That's the one thing we'll miss at the Champions Dinner at Augusta because Sam would always finish things off with a good ol' nasty story.

I played a few practice rounds with Sam and played in a few golf tournaments with him. It was a blast playing with him, like watching a fine piece of art. He had the soft hands and could really work the ball, and the day of working the ball is gone now. It's all power now. It was always great watching the older guys.

Adds **Zoeller***:*

Sam was very competitive when he fished, too. I can tell you that from my uncle.

John Mahaffey *got close enough to Sam and his nephew J. C. Snead to earn an invite to Sam's house while visiting J. C. in Hot Springs, Virginia:*

I was visiting J. C. in the off-season and we went over to Sam's house to visit him. Sam had remembered me a little bit because we had had the chance to play together a couple of times on the regular tour. He got this big ol' grin and he says, "C'mon, c'mon." And he took us down into his basement, where he had all kinds of stuff, including a lot of mementoes that a lot of people will never see, such as some of the old golf clubs with which he won tournaments and some of his old golf bags from Wilson. He also had a workshop where he did a lot of his own work on his golf clubs.

On his walls were a lot of photos of his from hunting, including safaris he had been on, such as in Africa, and he loved to talk about this. He talked about the time he rode the boat over to go play in the British Open. Just last year, we got a chance to talk down in Miami when J. C. and I did a clinic with Sam. He didn't hit many shots in the clinic, but he was a real character just talking and telling stories. It was shortly after that that he started to deteriorate.

While visiting him up there, I came to see it was one of the prettiest parts of the country I have ever seen. J. C.'s farm and Sam's farm are just gorgeous. If I took some time off to visit there for a while, I might never want to leave. Sam's view from his house is absolutely breathtaking with the mountains and the pastures, and the foliage in the autumn. I know J. C. and Sam always concentrated hard on the golf while they were out on tour playing, but they've got a great place to go to, to get relief from competing. That's part of the reason why Sam had such great longevity.

He had such a sweet swing, yet he wasn't into a whole lot of swing theory. To him it was just all about common sense, finding out what things would work and what wouldn't work when under the gun.

Lee Trevino *is one of the best at injecting humor and funny asides into a round of golf, but he would concede the top prize for public speaking to Snead:*

He was one of the best after-dinner speakers I've ever been around. He was like an old ballplayer who could tell you great stories from way back. A lot of that is because back in the early days of the tour, the guys would travel, room, and eat together, and they got to know each other really well, on and off the golf course. Nowadays, once a guy leaves the golf course, he doesn't see any of the other guys until they play again the next day.

Freddie Haas broke bread with Snead many times:

Sam Snead was probably the best dinner partner you could have. In the first place, he enjoyed good food, and he ate well. But he also always had a joke or two, and he could really keep a conversation going. He had a lot of interests, having been all around the world. It was wonderful to be able to spend an evening with Sam. He was the life of the party, and people loved being around him.

Sam had a fantastic memory, such as in being very grateful to Johnny Bulla. Johnny was going to play in the British Open, in 1946, and this was at a time when not too many (Americans) enjoyed playing in the British Open. That was mostly because you had to take a boat over there in those days, and it could be quite difficult getting over your sea legs.

But Johnny decided he was going to go, and because he was a great friend of Sam Snead's, he wanted some company in going over there with him. "C'mon, Sam," he said to Snead, "go over to the British Open with me." Sam said, "I don't want to go over there. Gosh, you can't make any money and you have to be gone three weeks just to play in it. I can't afford to do that."

Bulla kept after him and kept after him, and after a couple of months Sam finally agreed, and for all I know Johnny might have paid Sam's way over there. Well, Johnny finished second, and guess who won it? Snead. Absolutely.

Bob Toski:

Everyone knows that Sam was a storyteller. He loved to tell a story, and if you didn't laugh, he'd laugh. He was very congenial and outgoing. But one shortcoming people saw in him was that he didn't treat high-handicappers and poor players very well. He didn't have the patience to try to teach them how to play. Or if they didn't play fast enough or keep up with him, he felt they were just holding everybody up. He was much more compatible with you if you were a tour player, or at least a good player.

Sam was an amazing guy. One time we played in the Philadelphia Enquirer Open. On the tenth hole at White Marsh Valley, a long par-five, he was able to hit a one-iron uphill onto the green, straight in between a couple of bunkers and right up to within six feet of the hole. As we were walking up to the green, I said, "Sam, that was a great golf shot." Boy, that was something to watch.

As we continued to walk up to the green, there were two elderly ladies walking across the fairway about twenty yards in front of the green. One of the ladies looked at Sam and said to him, "Mr. Snead," as she pointed at the flag, "you're short." Sam walked over to the lady, tapped her on the shoulder, and said, "Yeah, I'm short. I'm short of sensational." Then he turned to me and said, "That dumb broad."

Toski:

I don't think enough people realize just what a warm, wonderful human being Sam was, and what a simplistic way he had for playing the game of golf and for teaching it. The game has lost one of the greatest legends who ever lived.

Longtime golf writer **Larry Dennis** *got to spend a lot of time with Snead when both were members of* Golf Digest's *pro panel, brainstorming and writing instructional articles for the magazines. Dennis found Snead to be an editor's delight in that Sam had such great recall of events from long ago, an asset which only helped the editorial process:*

Sam had a great memory. One time I had watched him play an exhibition back in Iowa, where I grew up. This had to be in the late fifties. Years later, after I had gotten to know Sam pretty well, I asked him if he ever remembered playing an exhibition in this small town, the name of which I can't remember now. "Oh, sure," he said. "In fact, I damn near got killed flying out of there," in a small plane. But he remembered the course, the town, and everything about it. This had to be about twenty-five years later.

Doug Ford *was a Snead crony who chips in with his own story of a visit to Hot Springs:*

Sam was a man's man. He was the greatest guy to be with, whether going out to dinner or spending some time at his house. One time while traveling with Ted Kroll (another golfer), we stopped in there on our way to somewhere, and we couldn't find his house. Finally, somebody told us that he lived opposite the airport. Once we got to his house, I told Sam, "Sam, what are you trying to do, save money by not turning any lights on? Couldn't you put at least one light on?"

The next morning after we got up, I asked Sam if we could go look at his supply of equipment in the cellar, and at first he wasn't going to let us. He finally let us go in there, and I think he still had, among a lot of other things, the first bag that Wilson ever gave him to use when he started working with them.

You know, he built that house around the safe he had taken from a bank that he bought in the town where he lived. He bought the bank, turned it into a restaurant, took their walk-in vault, and put it into the new house, a three-story house that he built into a hill. This was where he kept all his souvenirs and memorabilia. It was a beautiful room, and we kidded him that "You don't need to bury your winnings (in a tomato can) anymore; you can now lock it all away in that big safe."

Ford:

Sam wouldn't let you pick up a check if you went out with him.

He had a bad rep of hustling, but it really wasn't hustling because he was so damn good you couldn't beat him. And it's not like he was sneaking up on people who played against him. Take Greenbrier. Sam knew everyone's handicap there, but what they didn't know was that his handicap was like a plus-six or something like that. His average score there was about a 65, so whoever he played was dead before they started because Sam would play as a scratch.

Bob Goalby *was seventeen years younger than Snead and didn't meet him until the late fifties, but it wasn't long before they were chumming around together a lot, on and off the golf course:*

We both had the same interests. We liked to fish and we liked to hunt.

Sam was my idol before I ever thought of becoming a golf pro. He was a good player back in the thirties and forties, and I became a caddie in 1938, so naturally I started off reading a lot about Sam and all the pros. But there wasn't much coverage back then. What stories you could find were only about three to six inches long.

I was always a Snead fan. I was in the army with a nephew of his, a guy by the name of Homer Stinespring. I was stationed with him for a couple of years; in fact, I played on the Fourth Division football team with him. One time he said something about his Uncle Sam, and I said to him, "You're not by any chance talking about Sam Snead, are you?" He said, "Yeah, that's my uncle." Sam had one sister, and she had married a guy by the name of Stinespring.

I got talking to Homer and he told me, "Oh, Uncle Sam's a great guy. He gave me this '36 Ford Roadster with twelve coats of lacquer paint on it, and it has a '41 Mercury engine in it. He bought it out in California. Sam told me it would really run, and it could go about 110 miles per hour." It was all fixed up, with these superchargers on the side. Supposedly, Sam ended up giving the car to this kid.

Years later, I was up in northern Ontario near James Bay on a little lake, fishing with Sam out in a boat. This was after I had known Sam for about ten or twelve years, and in all that time I had never mentioned Homer Stinespring to him.

We were sitting in the boat, when I said to Sam, "You know, I've never told you this, but I used to be in the army with your nephew Homer Stinespring. He told me all about that '36 Ford Roadster with twelve coats of lacquer paint and superchargers on the side, with the '41 Mercury engine, that you gave him." Well, Sam jumped up in the boat, almost turning it over, almost drowning both of us. He said, "That little son of a b---- paid me fifteen bucks for that car, and he still owes me 825 dollars."

***J. C. Snead** remembers a time when it was Sam's turn to cool a hothead, in this case Goalby:*

Bob Goalby told me that he was a hothead when he first came on tour. Sam pulled him aside one day and said, "Boy, you're not hurting anybody but yourself. You need to do this, and you need to do that," and Bob won the next week. Bob and Sam were very close, and Bob would go down and check on Sam for the last ten years of his life to make sure he was okay.

***Bob Goalby** recalls how he met Snead and where the friendship went from there:*

I really met him when I won the Greensboro Open in 1957, when I birdied the last two holes to win. There was a five-way tie for second. At the presentation, I could hear Sam somewhere nearby saying, "Who in the hell is Goalby?" He was supposed to win in Greensboro, you know, because this was a tournament he would end up winning eight times. I was kind of standing off there in back waiting to get my trophy, and finally I said, "I am, Mr. Snead." And that's when I first met him and introduced myself.

After that, we got to be pretty good friends, and from about 1960 until he retired I played almost every practice round in any tournament in which we both played, including the U.S. Open and the Masters. All the senior tournaments, too. He played quite a bit on the regular tour in the sixties.

I spent four winters with him at Gleneagles, down on Delray Beach—we both had a condo on the golf course there. Then I spent three winters with him at Fort Pierce, and then I spent a lot of other time with him down in Florida. Those seven years in Florida I played almost every day with him. He got to where he wouldn't play unless he could play with me, because he didn't play as well anymore and didn't like playing with just anybody.

Mark Fry, *the director of golf schools at The Homestead, is young enough to have been Snead's grandson. But there was little, if any, generation gap between the two, who struck up a solid friendship in Snead's later years. It was a friendship that featured a lot of good golf instruction and knowledge being passed from one generation to another:*

Sam was a small-town guy, one of my idols. There's only forty-two hundred people in all of Bass County. Most people coming from small towns probably don't anticipate that they will really make something out of their lives. But then you look at a guy like Sam, who walked the same roads and drank the same water that you did, and look what he turned out to be—not only a national icon, but a worldwide-known person as well. That kind of thing gives you inspiration, no matter where you're from.

I would estimate that Bass County has produced fifty professional golfers over the years, and that's pretty amazing. Sam had to be a big inspiration for everyone who came behind him.

I had dinner with him quite often. He was just one of the guys. It's a proud moment when you can go into one of the Sam Snead's Taverns to have dinner with Sam and J. C., and everyone else in there is watching but probably wondering, *Who in the heck is that guy with Sam and J. C.?* The Taverns are a chain of restaurants, including one within walking distance of the resort that is operated by The Homestead.

Although Snead's small-town roots ran deep and tethered him close to his Virginia home, he still took advantage of his golf fame and success to become something of a world traveler. Longtime promoter **Fred Corcoran** *once recalled one such trip overseas:*

One year Sam and I were traveling through Europe, and he thought it would be a good idea if we had an "audition" with the Pope. I arranged it, and when we got ready to leave the hotel for the Vatican, I suggested that Sam bring along his putter and have it blessed. We were met in the vestry of Saint Peter's by a monsignor who proceeded to tell us that he was a 100 shooter who was having putting problems. Sam quickly put away the putter. "If you're that close to the Pope and you can't putt, he ain't gonna be able to do anything for me," he said.[8]

***Lee Trevino** debunks at least one myth about Snead:*

People always made of fun of Sam, because whenever he won another big payoff, he would always make reference to the fact that he was going to put the money in another tomato can to be buried in his backyard. He got that kind of talk stuck on him early in life, and he would keep playing off of that, talking about it as though he really did that.

One truth that a lot of people don't know about is that if they were to go to his hometown, they would find things like boys clubs and girls clubs that he has paid for without letting anybody know about it. He was a very generous man who had grown up very poor, and he didn't want to be poor again. He never wasted money—he was very conservative.

*If you were going to hang around Sam Snead, you had to have a thick skin and allow yourself to be kidded on occasion. **Johnny Bulla**:*

Sam always got on me about my hair because I always had a full head of hair, and he'd started losing his hair when he was in his twenties.

I came into the hotel one night and found him with a bath towel stretched out between the twin beds, and he was leaning over the towel breaking eggs and rubbing them on top of his head. I asked him what the hell he was doing, and he said, "I heard that your hair will grow if you rub raw eggs on your head." I just laughed.

Bob Goalby, *on one of the special privileges Snead got at Augusta, courtesy of Bobby Jones:*

I played a lot of practice rounds (at Augusta) with Sam, almost every year . . . for thirty years. One time we were going to twelve (a par-three over water) and crossing the bridge, when (Bobby) Jones drove up in his cart, with Cliff Roberts. They said, "Hello, Sam. How are you doing?" and this and that. . . . Being that we were at the bridge, Sam said to (Jones), "Hey, Bob, do you mind if I wet my line?" There were fish in the pond that you could see when you went around the par-three. Jones stood there a while, and finally he said, "All right, Sam, it would be all right, but don't keep them when you catch them. Throw them back in."[9]

Comedian **Bob Hope**, *speaking of being paired with Snead on occasion at the Phoenix Open pro-am:*

One year there was some minor international incident in Iraq—I just can't recall now what it was—and I happened to ask Sam, "What do you think of Iraq?" He looked at me and said, "I never played it. Who's the pro there?" Sam thinks Beirut is an after-shave lotion.[10]

Dan Quayle, *recounting the time in 1992 that, as Vice President, he hosted an eightieth birthday celebration for Snead, Ben Hogan, and Byron Nelson:*

My wife, Marilyn, and I were responsible for the seating arrangements for the dinner we hosted at the Vice President's residence at the Naval Observatory. Having been in Sam's company at many a dinner, I knew our guests were in for a treat. Sam would probably tell many of his old stories and some new ones—Sam was renowned for his stories. The more I thought about the prospect, the more I worried about the seating arrangements. Marilyn and I had placed Sam between her and Supreme Court Justice Sandra Day O'Connor. Before we sat down to dinner, I made Sam promise to behave himself.[11]

Veteran golfer **Al Besselink** *found Snead easy on the ears and the eyes:*

Sam had that hillbilly twang, and he loved to tell jokes. He was always wearing such nice clean clothes and that straw hat.

Golf Digest *editor* **Guy Yocom** *remembers one photo session with Snead in which Sam handled an embarrassing situation with comedy-club-caliber aplomb:*

A few years ago, *Golf Digest* wanted to compare old equipment with new equipment to discern how they are technically different in terms of the actual performance of clubs and balls.

Equipment manufacturers we talked to were enthused about this, and they even made a golf ball from the early sixties—same construction, materials, compression, and everything.

Then we got a hickory-shafted club, probably from the late twenties, that was still in good condition. Now we needed someone to test all this, and who better to do that than Sam Snead? After all, this was a guy whose career had spanned the entire breadth of this equipment evolution and different eras of golf.

So everything is in place, and we have a photographer ready to go. Sam understands the concept we are shooting for here, and he's enthused about it.

The photographer has Sam in his viewfinder, and Sam's all set to pull the trigger on this shot. Just before Sam takes the club away, the photographer steps away from the camera and says, "Whoa, Sam, just a minute. Stop." He walks up to Sam and whispers to him, "Sam, your fly is undone." Sam looked down and, as he zipped up his pants, he said, "A dead bird never falls out of the nest." That, I think, was Sam. He wasn't a self-conscious person, and his sense of humor was such that he could make fun of himself while making a raunchy joke. So he zipped up his pants, and then got on with it.

Snead loved nature and animals so much that he eventually ditched one of his first loves, hunting. **Doug Ford***:*

Talk about a guy who loved nature. He had a pond at the bottom of the hill, or mountain, on which he lived. He had a pet fish that would come up and eat out of his hand. One time when I was there, he had just come back from the vet with a duck that had needed some attention, and it had cost him thirty-five dollars to pay the vet. I said to him, "For pete's sake, Sam, why don't you just eat it? It would be cheaper."

Sam also had more machinery on his property than you could shake a stick at. He kept it all in this big barn. If I had had that much machinery myself, I could have built my own golf course. Bulldozers, backhoes, trucks, everything you need. And everything was as clean and as perfect as you could have it. He could run any of that machinery himself, because he told me how he had used it, such as the time that he had rebuilt some of his property after they had had a flood there.

The house sits up there on the hill beautifully, but there is a lot more land behind it. He used to go turkey hunting back there. The annual limit on turkeys was supposed to be two, but he told me how he would kill four and then use the bulldozer to go up there and bring them back with the front of the bulldozer lifted up so no one could see how many he had as he brought them back to the house.

Sam was always hunting or fishing. He was a real outdoorsman.

Ford:

Sam and I liked the same things. Bob Goalby, too. We were all of the same ilk—we weren't troublemakers; we were B.S. artists.

The Homestead's **Mark Fry**, *like Snead, also hails from Hot Springs, giving him some well-grounded insights into what made Sam tick:*

I knew Sam as a young kid, and I'm thirty-six years old now.

I grew up playing golf from the time I was eight. I first met Sam about twenty-five to thirty years ago. I became a pretty good player around the time I was eleven or twelve years old, and Sam said he thought I was going to be a decent player. I first played golf with him when I was about thirteen or fourteen. I don't remember any specific details from my having played golf with him, except that I played pretty well. Where I grew up, my house was only about a driver and a six-iron away from Sam's house.

Even then, twenty-five or thirty years ago, Sam was still playing a lot of tour golf, and so I didn't get to really see much of him back then. I didn't have a personal relationship with him at that time, except for saying hello or playing the occasional round with him here and there. I later moved to Roanoke, Virginia, but I moved back here about seven years ago. That's when I really got close to him, after I came back here to The Homestead as the director of instruction and the golf schools as well. We're a five-star resort here in the mountains. We are a resort similar to what Greenbrier is.

After I came back to The Homestead, I would see Sam hitting balls up at the golf school, where I was teaching most of the time. I would tee up balls for him sometimes and talk to him a lot, trying to get any information I could out of him. At first, I was a little apprehensive about approaching him, because there I was a young professional and he was such a legend. I didn't want to look like I was trying to impress him. But he made me feel very comfortable. He was just a country boy, same as me. We soon developed a very good relationship, just by me watching.

I videotaped his swing some and fitted him for some clubs, figuring out and showing him his specs. I don't think anyone had ever really done that for him before. I mean, he obviously knew how he wanted his clubs to look, but to be officially fitted was, I think, a new thing for him. I even videotaped my fitting him, and that's something I will have to look at for the rest of my life.

I remember him hitting a number of clubs that had just been handed to him. He was trying a bunch of drivers and what-not, and after a while I noticed that one of his clubs just didn't seem to be sitting right at address. So I asked him, "Sam, have you been fitted?" And he said, "Fitted?" He wasn't too concerned with the new technology, but obviously that hadn't mattered considering how successful he had been.

During the fitting, I got him to hit a bunch of balls off a deflection board, which marks where your club is hitting on the ground and where it should be hitting. We fitted him out at about two degrees flat, which with the old standards was about a fifty-eight-degree lie angle on the five-iron. As he hit these specific clubs, he'd say, "Yeah, that one looks right," and it would mark just perfectly in the center.

So he still had the eye after seventy or eighty years of golf. He was amazing. I don't think the results of this fitting were any great revelation to him. This was a guy who had once made his own clubs, and he knew what felt right to him and what he wanted things to look like. None of those exact numbers were that interesting to him, because he could have taken a broom and hit the ball solidly with that. But he certainly seemed interested in the whole process of being fitted.

***Fry** paints a picture of The Homestead and what it looked like when Snead stepped into the foreground:*

The Homestead is in the Allegheny Mountains, a mountainous area that is beautiful. The resort sits in the valley on Route 220, and it's an amazing fifteen-thousand-acre resort. The golf school area used to be the eighteenth hole, which is now a driving range that aims right toward The Homestead, a huge 527-room facility down below, where there's a large tower that you're shooting at. It's gorgeous.

I would see Sam up there many days, even when he was in his eighties and it might be ninety degrees outside, and he would be hitting two or three hundred balls at a time. There would be golf students much younger than him complaining about their aches and pains, and Sam would drive up in his golf cart getting ready to hit all those shots, and the complaining would stop. Even in the heat of the day, Sam wouldn't bat an eye about doing that. That's the lifestyle he knew, and that's what he wanted to do. It probably kept him healthy for so long. I attribute his longevity to the work ethic that he had.

While he was hitting all those balls, Sam would say, "If I could just pick up another twenty or thirty yards, I would still be back out there playing with those fifty-year-olds." He had ambition, and he thought he was still going back out there, even later in life. He never gave up.

I get all kinds of golf students, men and women, ranging in age from the thirties through the seventies. With a golf student in his or her seventies, you don't anticipate their being very flexible or being able to hit the ball very far. Then you get Sam Snead in his eighties, and it was just incredible to watch him at that age, even after he had become somewhat fragile, frail, to be swinging the club at about eighty miles an hour with his driver and hitting drives that probably flew about 220 yards in the air. He was like a machine, just one after another.

I would always tell the golf school students to watch his routine, because we talked about routines in the golf school. Sam always had the exact same routine for every shot, and the shots just resembled each other so well, including the trajectories.

Sam would attend some of the lunches we had with the golf school students. I once had a women's *Golf Digest* school, which had about twenty to twenty-five women here taking the school. I invited Sam to come to our sit-down dinner, and he obliged. He would always do that. Anytime I ever asked him to attend a function to sign autographs or something like that, he always accepted. I never got turned down once. I would go pick him up at his residence to take him to dinner, and he would be dressed up in his coat, tie, and hat, always dressed appropriately. He'd tell stories, even though sometimes they weren't lady-friendly, but he wouldn't mind telling them. The ladies got a kick out of it. He was fun.

Don Wade *got about as close to Snead as any golf writer could:*

An interesting thing about Sam is that he loved hunting and fishing. But as he got older, he stopped hunting altogether. He said, "I just don't have the heart for it anymore. I love to watch the deer and other wildlife come up around here." He just lost the taste for it.

Sam Snead as a tailor? Don't laugh, says **Bob Goalby**:

Sam said that when he was young, he wanted to be a tailor. His mother was a seamstress, and she taught him how to sew on buttons, shorten pants, and things like that. He used to alter his own clothes. I've seen him patch a hole in his clothes or fix a seam that has come loose. He liked doing that stuff.

Sam was pretty creative. He also had beautiful handwriting. When he signed a scorecard, he used those big beautifully scrolling S's and the "n-e-a-d" was just perfect. His scorecard was immaculate. He made the numbers real fancy and there was no mark out of line. It was beautiful just to have your card done by Sam. I've got some signatures of his that I have saved just to look at over the years. He had a lot of talent.

Either Snead didn't read the newspapers much to know what was going on in the world, or he acted like he didn't.
***Don Wade**:*

Back when Ronald Reagan was first elected President, the Republicans were just lampooning (Speaker of the House) Tip O'Neill. *Golf Digest* had done a piece on Vice President George Bush, and they said, "You know, we really ought to do something on Tip O'Neill."

I'm from Boston (O'Neill was from Massachusetts) and I got assigned the story. I called a friend of mine at the *Boston Globe*, and he set up an interview for me with Tip, the most powerful Democrat in the country. I then called Tip's office, and now that I think about it, I'm pretty sure the guy I spoke with was Chris Matthews (the current host of *Hardball*), who I think was working for Tip at the time. He said, "Look, you get ten minutes with the Speaker. He's very busy and doesn't have a lot of time." I said, "No problem."

I start talking with Tip, and he's going gangbusters. Forty-five minutes into this interview, he's telling stories about how he used to caddie for Bobby Jones, when Jones was at Harvard. All this stuff, and he's telling me how nervous he gets playing in pro-ams. I said, "Mr. Speaker, here you are, one of the most powerful men in the country; these other guys must be nervous playing with you."

"Let me tell you something, old pal, most of these guys don't even know who I am," he said to me. "Let me tell you a story. One time I was down at Pine Tree playing with Sam Snead and a couple of guys named Kelly. We're playing a ten-dollar nassau, which is a little steep for my blood. So Sammy nicks me pretty good.

"We go back to the clubhouse to have lunch, and now we're going to play gin. Now I'm a pretty good gin player; in fact, I'm one of the best. So I win everything back from Sam, plus a little more. We finish up, Sammy gets up, shakes my hand, and says, 'O'Brien, you're a helluva fellow. What did you say you do for a living?'"

Longtime photographer ***Leonard Kamsler*** *has photographed many of the game's top players over the years, although his first brush with Snead didn't go so well:*

One year at the Masters, I had the assignment to get a picture of Sam. I don't remember what the exact reason for the assignment was, but I went up to Sam, introduced myself, and said I needed to get a photograph for *Golf* magazine. Sam looked at me and said, "*Golf* magazine? Ain't no way in the world I'm going to do anything for them. They wrote in some book that I 'psyched out Hogan.'"

Well, there I was with the assignment, and here's Sam bluntly and irrevocably pronouncing that he will not do it.

So, I went back that evening and saw the editor who had assigned me the story. I said, "What was it that you all did to Sam Snead, man? He doesn't want to have anything to do with you. He said something about your saying that he 'psyched out Hogan.'"

The editor says to me, "Leonard, we haven't done a piece on Sam in a long time. However, I do think we reviewed his book. This story about psyching out Hogan was in his book, that *he* wrote."

That was Sam. Maybe he hadn't read the book, although I don't remember which of his books it was.

When I started shooting golf, which had to be in the early sixties, most of the guys were pretty accessible. Sam came from an old school that was very leery of photographers. I had always heard, "Watch out for Sam." Over the years I followed him a fair amount, and I never had any trouble with him, except for that one time. Aside from that, he was pretty reasonable.

Don Wade *offers this story of mistaken identity, something which seemed to happen to Snead throughout his career:*

One day Sam called me up from Florida for something, and I said, "How are you doing? Are you playing any golf?"

"No. I'm still fishing."

"Are you having any luck?"

"No. You know what happened to me today? I was out there behind the house fishing, and I had a baseball cap on instead of my straw Panama hat. There's this old bird looking at me, looking me up and down, up and down, up and down. Finally, he comes over to me and says, 'You're somebody famous, aren't you?' 'Well, I believe, uh, that you might recognize me.' 'You're a golfer, right?' 'That's right.' 'I knew it! You're Ben Hogan. You're my hero. Can I have your autograph?'"

Sam said, "That ruined my whole day."

J. C. Snead *recalls being paired with his famous uncle in tour events, as well as how competitive the Sneads could be at almost anything:*

I was paired with him in the last round at Oakland Hills when he almost won the PGA Championship while in his sixties. The next year he was paired with me at Canterbury, and I finished third. I think those were the only two times we were paired in a major championship.

He would later laugh about that PGA, saying that he thought I was so interested in what he was trying to do and almost winning that I had forgotten that I was even playing. It was funny that the year I had a chance to win, he was miffed because he wasn't playing well and I was beating him. He didn't like that. But he was a competitor, and that's why he played so well for so long. That's what he said down at the Legends this year (2002), "Every time I played, I wanted to kill everybody."

If we played pool or anything, God almighty, it was like a war. One night we were playing pool at his house, and this was back sometime in the late sixties, and neither one of us could play very well. I said something smart at one point, and he said, "Okay, do you want to play for fifty cents?" And I said, "Why don't we just make it a dollar."

Well, he usually went to bed at eight or nine o'clock at night, and here it is 1:30 in the morning and I've got him down eight bucks, and he wasn't going to quit, not until his wife came down and ran the both of us off. It was the same thing playing marbles or anything. If we were fishing, the contest was to see who would catch the first fish, and then it was to see who would catch the biggest fish. In hunting, it was the biggest deer or the one with the most points. That's why he was a winner.

J. C. *is regretful about some things involving his uncle's career and how circumstances perhaps could have been different:*

If he had still been just fifty years old out here when the Senior PGA Tour got started, everyone else would have been playing for second place about every week. If the USGA had left him alone and allowed him to putt between his legs, he might have won a couple more tournaments. But they didn't like him either.

I've said this all along: It's a damn shame that the writers and people couldn't have said these nice things about him while he was still alive. I knew all along that everyone would wait until he died before they would say some nice things about him. I guess that's the way it goes.

A couple of weeks before he died was the last time I saw him, and everything seemed fine. I met him at the door of his house, and he was still acting like I was going to give him a friendly punch or something. You know, he used to box a little bit. We must have spent a couple of hours together that last time. He would start to say something, and it was just like it would go away. He couldn't remember.

The sad thing was that as I got up to go home, he said, "Where are you going?" We'd been watching the tournament

PHOTO COURTESY OF SUZIE SNEAD

The look on Sam's face suggests that he has just spotted another "pigeon."

at Hilton Head on television, and he was sitting up real close to the TV so that he could see it. Justin Leonard won the tournament, but when this other kid in contention made a double bogey at the sixteenth, Sam sat back and said, "What in the hell is he doing? What's that boy's name? What's he doing?" Sam was all upset.

When he said, "Where are you going?" I told him that I was going home. He looked at me real funny and kind of leaned over to me and said, "Where's home?" Then he asked me about this girl from Atlanta named Marilyn that I had been engaged to. "Are you going to call her? Are you going to call Marilyn?" It's like his mind was in and out. Then I left.

Later on I didn't realize that he had gotten that bad. I was going to play in New Jersey and then Michigan before going back home. They called me in Michigan after he had passed away. I got the first flight out that I could get home.

Earlier in the year at the Legends, we had sat together at a table, and he was okay even if he wasn't great. Get him a rum and coke and he would tell a few little stories. He was fine, but I could see that he was fading. I think he was having a bunch of these little ministrokes. But he had a great life and accomplished a lot of great things in the world of sports. He traveled the world and met kings. He even had an audience with the pope. I mean, what a life! It was full.

Johnny Bulla *spent many days and nights in a car with Sam Snead traversing the U.S. of A. to play in tournaments, and he would sometimes sense some sadness in Sam:*

Sam didn't have a really happy life, and there's two reasons for that. One is that he never won the U.S. Open and always had to live that down. The other was that he really wanted to have a good family life, but he didn't. I won't go much into that, except to say that his second son, Terry, was diagnosed as a little boy with some kind of brain damage. I don't know what happened, but Terry never was able to attain an adult mentality.

Jack Snead, *Sam's son, talked to writer Guy Yocom about why Sam, even at eighty-six years old, was so excited about a nine-hour car ride from his winter home in Fort Pierce, Florida, to Augusta for the 1998 Masters:*

People have a hard time believing it, but Dad gets lonely. He'll play solitaire by the hour at a pine table in his home in Hot Springs, and there's a spot on the table near where the deck sits that's worn down from his stroking the cards off the pile. This trip is good for him. He loves going to the Masters.[12]

Life on the road as a touring pro could be lonely, but the money had to be made so that bills back home could be paid. **Al Besselink***:*

A friend of mine in Nashville asked me one time about putting on a pro-am there. I told him, "If I was going to put on a tournament, I would get one man to give you a name, and I can get you that one man—Sam Snead." So I told this guy that he needed to pay Sam such and such an amount, give me some money under the table, and get Sam a broad. It was a good tournament, and we put it on for several years.

Writer **Larry Dennis** *was among those who were around the tour enough to see how Sam wouldn't try to hide the fact that he had female friends away from home:*

Sam was a notorious womanizer, and he never really made much of a secret of it. He left Audry at home, and he'd go out wherever he was going. I had breakfast one morning with Sam and one of his girlfriends in Chicago during the Western Open—he was traveling with her at the time.

Five or six years ago I ran into Sam at the PGA Merchandise Show in Orlando. I was editor of *Senior Golfer* at the time, and I had my daughter with me—she was our office manager. She's a pretty good-looking woman who was then in her thirties. We were walking across the lobby of the convention center, and here comes Sam. So I stopped, said hi, and introduced him to my daughter. After that, Sam didn't pay any attention to me; he only had eyes for my daughter. By this time he was in his early eighties. He was incorrigible.

Al Besselink saw Snead as someone whose pluses far outnumbered his minuses, beginning with Sam's generosity over the years:

One time I opened up a driving range in Philadelphia, and I said, "Sam, I'd like you to come out and give a little clinic." He said okay. But when he got there, he said he didn't want to hit any shots off those mats we had, so he moved his balls to in front of the mats, where it was like cinders and the lie was downhill. He put the balls on those cinders and never missed a shot.

Sam would sometimes mention to me that he had an exhibition coming up the next week, and he would give me five hundred to play with him. That was a lot of money, and Sam always had cash. He didn't want any checks. So I played many exhibitions with Sam Snead.

***Tommy Bolt**:*

Some people called Sam a tightwad, but those are people that didn't know him.

*Golfer **Bob Toski** interjects with this assessment of Snead's taste for competition, which was so intense that many players are sure Sam went to his grave looking for another game:*

Name the player who played the game competitively longer and better than Sam Snead. So who would be the best player of the twentieth century? Sam liked to play competitively, but we also had to play longer and better because we didn't make enough money to be able to retire. You think Tiger Woods will play that long competitively? He won't have to.

Sam had the desire to play and compete, and it wasn't just the money—it was also pride. You tell Sam you want to play a hundred-dollar nassau, and he'll put his drawers on faster than you can shake a stick at. He liked to hustle. He liked to compete and make money because that's how he had to make money. Take a look at Arnie (Palmer): he can't break an egg now. I can beat Arnold now. I think I'm the best seventy-five-year-old player in the country right now, except maybe for Joe Jimenez. He and I are neck and neck. If you know of two guys seventy-five years old who want to tee it up against Joe and me, grab your money and give me a call.

Don Wade *remembers how Sam's past acquaintances, as well as friendly strangers, would seem to come out of the woodwork while he was visiting Sam in Hot Springs:*

One time back at Hot Springs, he and I were having dinner at his original Sam Snead's Tavern. This woman comes up, probably in her sixties, and she says, "I apologize for interrupting you, but my husband and I are your biggest fans. Would you give us an autograph?"

Sam gets a pen out and gives her his autograph, this work of magnificent handwriting, just beautiful penmanship. After Sam signs the piece of paper, the woman takes it and she's all excited, and she says, "Thank you so much, Mr. Brewer. We are your biggest fans, and we look for you every year at the Masters." She thought she was getting Gay Brewer's autograph.

About a half-hour later, as we were finishing up dinner, all of a sudden some guy walks in the front door. Sam gets up and goes right over to get the guy and brings him over. He says, "Junior, this is so-and-so"—I can't remember his name, although I remember so well how this guy was built like a walking fire hydrant. Sam says to me, "This is my high school football coach." I'm thinking, *You've got to be kidding—this guy has got to be a hundred years old!*

Sam and his old coach start talking, and we head up to the second floor of the restaurant. The whole place was filled with Sam's memorabilia, and up on the second floor they had all this stuff from when Sam was in high school, playing football, basketball, and stuff. It was a sight to see.

***Wade*:**

Another time we were down playing at The Homestead, and I had one of those old JP II Wilson sand wedges, which was a heckuva club. They brought them out in the early eighties. Sam looked at it and told me, "You know, Junior, this is a pretty good pitching wedge, but it's not much of a sand club. When we get back to the house, let's see what we can find for you."

After we get back to his house, we go down to his workshop. He must have had every bag that had ever been given to him by Wilson. He's rummaging through all of these bags full of clubs and ends up bringing out about six Wilson Staff wedges, which at that time were the best wedges you could get. He's checking them out, doing this and that, and he hands me this one wedge and tells me to take it back to Connecticut with me.

He tells me, "If you can use it, keep it. If you can't, send it back and I'll send you another one."

All this time I'm thinking, *What are the chances of my ever even using this club? This is a keepsake.*

Four or five years ago, my youngest son, Andy, who would have been about nine or ten at the time, was taking golf camp at this club we belong to up here in Connecticut. One day he did the best among all the camp's golfers at something, and they gave him a collector's card that featured Sam Snead, like a baseball card. He came home so excited and asked, "Dad, do you think if we sent this to Mr. Snead that he would sign it for me?" I said, "Tell you what, we'll call him tonight and ask him."

So I called up Sam, and knowing that he would start out with a couple of risqué jokes, I told Andy to wait until I told him to pick up the phone to listen in. I told Sam what we wanted, and he told me to "put young Andrew on the phone."

Andy gets on the phone and he's nervous, and Sam tells him, "You dad tells me that you're a good golfer. Is that true?" And Andy just kind of says, "Uhhhh, yeah." Sam says, "You go to work on that short game and keep working on your putting, and don't just keep hitting the driver all the time like your old man does. Andrew, you send me that card, and I'll send it right back."

Andrew sent the card down to Sam, and it came back about a week later, signed by Sam and accompanied by a letter from Sam, on his stationery, to Andy.

J. C. Snead *didn't think having the Snead name was all that it was cracked up to be:*

There wasn't much good to it other than learning things from him. Financially, having the Snead name didn't help me at all. In fact, Sam once told me, "You would have done a lot better if your name had been Smith or Jones, just anything but Snead." I don't even have a club contract. I have nothing. I've had one contract since I've been on the Senior Tour (since 1990). That was with Callaway, although I couldn't play their equipment and quit. I tried real hard but just couldn't play it. The best thing for me to do was give them back their money and quit.

At times it's like I was the plague or something. When I started playing well, having Snead for a last name actually kind of worked in the wrong direction. Everybody figured I already had a contract with Wilson because Sam had been with Wilson for so long. I ended up with Wilson for a little while and then was with Northwestern for ten or twelve years. But exhibitions and endorsements coming my way have been very, very sparse.

J. C. *speaks on behalf of his uncle in lamenting how Sam's PGA Tour career victory total started dropping long after he had left the regular tour:*

Sam was upset because Beman (former PGA Tour Commissioner Deane Beman) took away the official status of some of his tournament wins. He had eighty-seven at one time, and then all of a sudden it went to eighty-two.

One of the tournaments they took away was one that was played in Canada. They played two tournaments in Canada, and Byron Nelson won one during his eleven-tournament winning streak. Sam won another one just like it, but they later took his win away in terms of official tour status, but they never took Byron's away. Few people really know about that, and until he got really old, Sam didn't complain about it. He said, "Geez, Jack Nicklaus isn't going to win another tournament, but before this is all over he's going to pass me on the all-time win list."

I tell people, yeah, I'm prejudiced, but he was my uncle and my best friend.

***Jack Vardaman**, Sam's attorney friend from Washington, D.C., intervened on Sam's behalf in regard to the number of Sam's career victories:*

Until 1968, the tour was run by the PGA of America, which kept its own records, including who won how many tournaments. Some years later the PGA Tour published its history of the PGA Tour. They sought to reexamine tournament wins, and they took away from Sam eight tournament wins that the PGA of America had always credited Sam with. He thought it was unfair and I agreed with him.

In 1996 I wrote to Commissioner (Tim) Finchem and I asked, "How can you take away eight tournaments from Sam that the PGA of America recognized and gave him credit for, when they were the body that ruled golf at the time?" It would be like the commissioner of baseball now saying, "We're going to take away some of Babe Ruth's home runs because the ballparks were too small," or the NFL saying, "We're going to rewrite the history of the AFL before the merger."

You would think that the PGA Tour would accept the PGA of America's characterizations. But those eight tournaments that the PGA of America credited to Sam aren't among the eighty-two for which he is given credit today by the PGA Tour. I wrote a long letter to Tim Finchem pointing this out and got a nice letter back from (another PGA Tour official), but nothing ever happened.

__Vardaman__ became close friends with Snead over the latter's last twenty years, and they would get together for a few days in Augusta during Masters week:

Sam had a terrible automobile accident one year driving to Augusta. He got sued, and I helped him out in the lawsuit. After that, he would always give me tickets to the Masters, and I would rent a house in Augusta. Sam would come in on Tuesday around midday, and he would stay with me until he left, generally on Thursday. He would go to the Champions Dinner on Tuesday night, play in the Par-Three on Wednesday, hit the first shot on Thursday, and then leave for Hot Springs.

I would sometimes go out on the practice tee with Sam. As we walked out there, two things would happen: Any number of players would stop what they were doing to just come up and shake his hand and say, "Mr. Snead, it's an honor to meet you, or to see you." It really was a wonderful thing to see these great players pay homage to the man who had done so much for the game. The other thing, when Sam would start to hit balls, they would all stop and watch, even this past year, when he was eighty-nine years old. (Nick) Faldo and (David) Leadbetter would come over and take films. He still had what was called by many the best swing in golf, and the group marveled at it.

PHOTO COURTESY OF JACK VARDAMAN

Snead is joined by attorney-friend Jack Vardaman in front of the clubhouse at Augusta National Golf Club.

***Vardaman** helped represent Sam in a lawsuit that was brought by the paralyzed driver of the other car involved in the 1992 auto mishap that was ruled Sam's fault, with a multi-million-dollar settlement reportedly reached a few years later:*

Sam felt terrible about it because the man was seriously injured. He had a very heavy heart as a result of that. Sam also injured his left shoulder quite badly, and that took a lot of Sam's strength away.

*Writer **Guy Yocom** recalls the time in 1998 when he arranged with Snead to do a story from the standpoint of accompanying Sam for the nine-hour ride from Snead's winter home in Fort Pierce, Florida, to Augusta for the Masters. The drive itself was eventful, but not for the right reasons:*

It was downright scary, from the outset. In the first place, I was only half-awake in that car starting out. We left the house at some ungodly hour like 4:30 or 5:00 in the morning. It was awful, and those guys were wide awake. Remember, these guys are from the hills of Virginia, and this is normal for them. I had had a long flight into West Palm the night before and had then driven all the way up to Fort Pierce, and I was tired. I had had only a few hours of sleep.

I'm in the backseat of this car, and what happened was that Sam started slurring his words. Something wasn't right. At first he was talking, making some inane comments about some of the cars or whatever that we saw along the way. Jack noticed that something wasn't right. By the time we got up to Jacksonville, now it was rush hour and it was really busy with traffic there on I-95.

Suddenly Sam says, "I'm going to be sick." Jack whipped the car over to the emergency lane, and in a few seconds we're all out of the car and Sam is throwing up, and he's as white as a ghost. It was surreal, and I was even thinking, *This legend could die right in front of me*. It was really harrowing, and we still had a long way to go to get to Augusta. But Sam was feeling a little better and he refused to go to a hospital. It was a real tense deal for the rest of the trip, except for Sam. He just wanted to get up there.

Doug Ford *recalls Snead's last few years:*

His memory was amazing. Even when he was almost ninety years old, he could tell you joke after joke. The last time I played golf with him was at Fort Pierce in Florida, where he was the director of golf. His eyes were gone. He couldn't recognize you if you were three feet from him.

Don Wade recalls how Snead's resolve and loyalty never left him:

I remember that while he was living in Florida, there was a development that had gotten guys like Sam and Bob Goalby involved in this condominium. They might even have given him a condo to stay in.

I believe it was for Sam's eightieth birthday that they gave him a big party at Pine Tree over in Boynton Beach, and as a gift they gave him this beautiful golden retriever named Meister. Sam's wife, Audry, passed away right around that time, and Sam became very attached to Meister. Meister would sit in the golf cart with Sam and they would drive around together. Meister was a great dog.

Of course, Sam took Meister to live with him at this development down in Florida. The owners came to him and said that they had received some complaints from other owners about his having Meister out on the golf course. They just weren't going to allow that. Sam simply said, "If this place isn't good enough for Meister, it's not good enough for me." And he packed up and moved out of there.

***Guy Yocom**, added the following coda to Snead's career, describing in* Golf Digest *Sam's arrival one year on the first tee at Augusta as an honorary starter, following Gene Sarazen and Byron Nelson:*

The applause for Sam is prolonged, and trebled in volume. Sam tips his hat, walks forward, and tees his ball. He sidles alongside the ball, waggles beautifully—he always had the most beautiful waggle in the game—and cocks an eye down the fairway. Then it is as if an angel enters Sam's body, for he wheels away from the ball like the Slammer of old, his right shoulder stretching behind him, his left arm jutting into the sky. He pauses distinctly at the top and brings the club down like the arm of a locomotive. *Pow!* The ball explodes off the clubface like a bullet, arcing high and far toward the distant fairway bunker on the right. At the last moment it turns over and returns to earth, coming to rest in the exact middle of the center mowing stripe, 230 yards away. There is a moment of paralyzed silence, and then thunderous, sustained cheers shatter the morning. People jump, scream, back-pound, and high-five each other. The fellow standing next to me shakes his head and his voice breaks as he mutters, "Unbelievable. . . . Unbelievable." He looks at me with tears in his eyes, and he isn't ashamed.[13]

6

SLAMMER THE GAMER

As much as Sam Snead loved golf, it really wasn't a recreational outlet for him. It was rarely a time for him to relax, admire the scenery, and smell a few roses along the way. He loved the game, for sure, but he loved the gaming even better. Strangers could become playing partners if they were willing to open their wallets and be upfront about stating their handicaps.

When Snead first started playing the tour in the late thirties, purse money was sparse. Only a handful of golfers in tournaments could really make enough to cover expenses, so the income had to be supplemented in other ways. There were, of course, the off-season club-pro jobs at resorts and country clubs, but all that did was pay some bills and did little for fueling the competitive fires.

There was real money to be made on those days between tournaments during tour season, as well as when their schedules back at their home clubs allowed them to get out and play eighteen holes here and there with varying amounts at stake in nassaus. This was a big part of what constituted gambling in golf, and Snead loved every minute of it. He didn't lose very often, and when he did it sometimes took some extra checking on amateurs' backgrounds to see if they were being honest about asking for strokes.

Practice-round money games remain a part of the PGA Tour landscape, but there's no way they are played today with the kind of gusto and, at times, desperation that characterized the "friendly wagers" made fifty or sixty years ago. It usually cost money to play golf with Sam Snead, but the payback was four hours of highlight-reel golf featuring one of the greatest players of all time, as well as being privy to some of the best storytelling you would ever want to hear (or, in some cases, not want to hear).

***Doug Ford** was one of Snead's frequent playing partners, and there's no doubt in Ford's mind that playing golf with Snead and handing over some greenbacks helped his own career, which included victories in two majors:*

Even though he wasn't what I would call well educated, Sam had become friends with many CEOs. Anybody who knew him and played golf with him could call him his friend, even if he stole all their money out on the golf course.

He used to come up to the Masters every year and he would have a roll (of cash) that you could choke a horse with, with a bunch of hundred-dollar bills. This was money he had won during the winter while down at his job in Boca Raton. If you played Sam and he beat you, you had to pay him on the eighteenth green. If you beat him, you'd have to look for him up in the men's room.

There was one time in 1968 when we were playing a practice round at Augusta, and we were behind Ralph Guldahl. Ralph, most likely, was the best player in the thirties. I knew that Sam had years earlier been partners in the Miami Four-Ball with Ralph, and I said to him, "You know, Sam, I never see you talk to Guldahl at dinner or in any way be friendly with him."

Sam stopped dead still, took his wallet out, and pulled out a folded piece of paper about an inch square. He opens it up, shows it to me, and it says, "I O U sixteen hundred dollars, Ralph Guldahl." Guldahl had borrowed that money from Sam way back in 1939, and here it is about thirty years later and he's still carrying the IOU around with him.

Bob Goalby *could often be found playing with Ford and Snead in the sixties and some in the seventies:*

Most people didn't want to play with him anyway because they were afraid he was going to hustle them, when in fact you have to say, "How in the hell is he going to hustle anyone?" It's not like they didn't know how good he was already and that they had their handicaps to use in playing against him anyway. How do you get hustled by someone who you already know was once the best player in the world? A hustler is someone who says he's a twelve when he's actually about a six.

I know two people from Saint Louis who were once at The Greenbrier and called me, asking if I could get a game for them with Sam, that they would be willing to give him a bet. I called Sam and happened to get him, and I told him about the two guys wanting to play him. He said, "Yeah, I'll play with them, Bob. What do you want me to do, to call them or are they going to call me?" I said, "Sam, why don't you call them because they're too scared to call you."

So he called them and gave them a game, giving them two more than their handicaps after I had told him they were legit. Well, he shot something like a 64 and beat the hell out of them, winning a couple hundred apiece from them. But that's no big deal, because when you play with the best player in the world you've got to expect to pay. If you spend four hours with the best lawyer in the world, you know it's going to cost you more than two hundred. The next day, Sam gave them four more than their handicaps, and they lost another couple hundred. But they called me and told me how it had been the greatest time in their lives, and they thanked me again for getting them hooked up with Sam.

About six months later, another guy in Saint Louis I know came up to me and said, "Your damn friend Snead hustled my two friends," and then named the two guys that I had set Sam up with. I said, "What are you talking about? They called me asking for the game, and I made the arrangements." That's how those stories about Sam hustling (unwitting) people get blown out of proportion.

There was another time in Boca Raton, where these two guys from up in New York saw Sam practicing, and they went up to him and said, "We'd like to play with you. I'm an eleven and my friend here is a twelve, and we'd like to have a little game." Well, one guy shoots something like a 37 or a 38, and they ended up winning a couple hundred from Sam.

About eight to ten years later, Sam's back up at The Greenbrier practicing and getting ready to play, when these two guys walked out on the range and said they'd like to have a game. Sam recognized them, when they thought he wouldn't. This time he asked them exactly where they were from, and he figured he was going to play their game now.

So Sam called the pro at their club, a guy he knew very well, and said, "Hey, I've got two of your boys here and they got me pretty good for some money about ten years ago. I want to know what their handicaps are." The pro told Sam, "Well, one guy is a six and he can play to it, and the other guy is a seven, but sometimes he can't play to it."

The next day they came back out and Sam, pointing to the guys, said, "Okay, you're going to get six and you're going to get seven." And they said, "Oh, no, no, no. We're a twelve and a thirteen." Sam said, "Nope, this is what you get. I called your pro and that's what your handicaps are." Well, they played and Sam skinned them real good.

There's always someone trying to hustle Snead, too. That story goes two ways, but no one ever hears about the times guys pull one over on him. There was always somebody laying for him. Of course, Sam once confided to me, "I never told them I was a plus-four at the Old White," which is a course up at The Greenbrier. But it was an honor to play with him, certainly worth that fifty or seventy-five dollars you might lose playing him. It was a cheap lesson for four hours of being able to watch a golf ball get massaged so beautifully.

Sam was tough. Even the other pros would say, "You can't beat the guy." Head to head he was tough, until he got to where he couldn't putt very well, and that's when you could beat him.

You didn't have to be a pro golfer or belong to Snead's inner circle of friends to get a game with the great one. Writer **Don Wade** *teed it up with Snead on numerous occasions:*

Typically, when I went down there to do a story, I would work with Sam a little bit and then we would go to play some golf. Everyone always said that when you played with Sam, you played better because you got into his rhythm. I don't think that's true. My experience with Sam was that he was so beautiful to watch play, that, invariably, by trying to get into his rhythm, it would get you out of yours.

But he was wonderful to play with. We used to have a bet, and this is going back fifteen to twenty years when Sam was into his seventies. He would give me two strokes on the front side and then we'd adjust on the back. At the time, I was a single-digit handicapper. The bet with Sam would usually be ten-dollar nassaus, but with a twist. It would be ten on the front, ten on the back, and twenty overall. He figured you might get lucky and beat him on one side or the other, but you probably weren't going to beat him overall.

He was great, too, because he would never give you any advice as long as the bet was still alive. But once he closed you out, he might tell you something. One time while playing down at the Lower Cascades Course, he closed me out on seventeen. So we were playing eighteen, and I'm getting ready to hit my approach shot. He says, "You know, Junior, you've got about six good swings. Why don't you pick one of them and stick with it?" That was wonderful advice. What I had been doing, perhaps subconsciously, was mimic his swing.

Another time when we were playing down there, there's a par-five hole that plays sort of downhill and is reachable in two. Sam hit it in two, and I hit it down to the right and into the rough, and I had to come back up over a bunker. I hit a really good shot and the ball ended up dead to the hole. Sam, standing up on the green, threw down his putter, and said, "Damn it, Junior, you're not that good." It was great playing with him.

Likewise, ***Guy Yocom*** *got a chance to put down pen and pad long enough to match shots with Snead:*

The first time I was actually with Sam was in around 1985. It was the grand opening of a golf course down in south Florida where several legends, including Sam, had each contributed a hole or two to the design.

It was actually a media event, and they had set it up so that the writers would get a chance to play the course with these various legendary golfers. The format was that each writer would play with two of these legends, one for the first nine holes and the other guy for the second nine.

I drew Sam to play the front nine, and this was going to be a highlight of my life because this guy is my hero. I was pretty excited about this, although I could tell that Sam was half-bored because this wasn't his idea of fun—there's no action. He's basically camping out. But knowing that Sam liked to bet, and that that might bring him to life a little bit, I said, "Sam, let's have a little bet. Let's play for something. You want to play for twenty bucks?"

That got his attention. He cocked his ears, turned around, and said, "What's your handicap?" I was about a five, but I told him that I wanted five strokes—for the nine holes. You've got to remember that even then, Sam was probably something like a plus-two or plus-three when it came to handicaps. On top of that, this is his golf course. Home-course advantage, you know? Five shots for me was reasonable for nine holes. Actually, it was a bit beyond reasonable, but I suppose I was trying to bait him a little bit. I was hoping he would come back at me and say, "I think we should negotiate or something." But he said, "Yeah, okay, I'll give you five shots, No problem."

We play the front nine, and I shoot like a 39. That's pretty good for me. Sam shoots a 36. At the end of the nine holes, I said to him, "Thanks very much, Sam, but it looks like I got you by two." And he said, "What are you talking about?"

I said, "Well, you gave me five shots, and I had a 39 to your 36, so I got you for the twenty dollars, right?"

He said, "Well, what about the back nine?"

"Sam, we're not playing the back nine. This is nine holes. I gotta go play the second nine with someone else now"—it might have been Doug Ford or Billy Casper, I'm not sure which.

He said, "You mean I'm not playing all eighteen with you?"

"No."

He just looked at me, stomped down on the gas pedal of his golf cart, and drove off. As he drove off, he said, to me, "Well, next time we'll just have a better understanding." So he drove off with my twenty dollars.

Larry Dennis *recalls how golfers who had at one time beaten Snead in an important competition could make the Slammer chafe at the mention of such an event:*

Sam did have a bit of a temper. At one of our panel meetings, we were just sitting around and talking about a variety of subjects. Paul Runyan was also on the panel at that time, and Paul never missed an opportunity to remind Sam about the time that he had whipped Snead, in a match-play encounter, at the PGA Championship back in the late thirties. "Little Poison," that's what they called Paul.

Sam was outdriving Paul by fifty yards, but Runyan was a genius with his fairway woods and around the green. And Paul would never neglect to tell Sam about how he had beaten him in that match. Sam wouldn't say much, but you could see that he was apoplectic. You could just see it—the veins in his neck were bulging.

***Dennis** also had the privilege of playing with Snead:*

One of the highlights of my career, probably in the early eighties, was at one of our pro panel meetings at a course in Massachusetts. One afternoon we went over to The Country Club in Brookline, and I was paired with Sam for a round of golf.

He wasn't playing very well for the first two or three holes, but finally on the fourth hole he cranked one off the tee pretty well. I then hit, and I cranked a pretty good shot myself, with my ball coming to rest about two or three yards behind his. I then hit my second shot to about twelve to fifteen feet from the hole. Sam turned around to me and said, "What did ya hit?" And I never thought that the day would come when Sam Snead would ask me what I had hit on a hole.

There were plenty of lighter moments when it came to playing golf with Snead, even with money at stake. As great a golfer

Bob Goalby and Sam Snead look dapper in tuxedoes in 1986 while filming a TV commercial in Los Angeles.

Photo courtesy of Bob Goalby

and shotmaker as Snead was, he had rabbit ears and an inquiring mind. He was always wanting to know what others in his group were hitting for their shots, and he could sometimes be influenced into picking the wrong club out of his bag. **Doug Ford**, *who won the Masters Tournament in 1957, recalls one particular time playing Augusta with Snead:*

I played a lot of games with Snead there. I can remember on the second hole (a par-five), one day, where he took his driver and poured it over the hill and then knocked it onto the green. The next day while going to the second tee, I turned to (Bob) Goalby and said, "I'm going to hit a three-wood off the tee here. Ask me why, because Snead has rabbit ears, you know." I then said, a bit louder, "I wouldn't take a chance here, because if you go a little left, you're talking six or seven. I'll just lay back and then try going at the green with my third shot."

I get up there and hit my three-wood, and Goalby steps up and hits his three-wood, and then Snead gets up there, goes with his three-wood (instead of driver), and he duck-hooks it into the trees, from where he made something like an eight. That was pretty funny. You've got to really think and play the right shot off the tee at Augusta.[1]

Ford *expounds further on Sneads management of club selection.*

If you said something around Sam, with his rabbit ears, you could change his train of thought. I remember playing a practice round with him and Bob Toski at Jacksonville. When we were going down the seventeenth fairway to hit our second shots, I turned to Toski and whispered, "Let's give him the business. I'm going to hit a nine-iron and you hit an eight-iron." And this was with Sam's ball about five yards in front of us.

I hit my nine and Toski hit his eight, and now Sam doesn't have any idea what to hit because he's paying so close attention to what we hit. Finally, he takes his nine and air-mails the green.

I think Sam was so concerned about what other people were hitting because I don't think he had enough confidence in his club selection. I told him one time that if I had caddied for him he would have won three hundred tournaments. I said, "You listen to everybody instead of believing in yourself." As great a player as Sam was, he didn't always believe in himself. I said to him, "You listen to this guy and to that guy, and you know *ten* times what they know."

Sam had a great caddie for a long time by the name of Cemetery, who was out of Pinehurst. Sam had a lot of confidence in him, and one time Sam sent Cemetery to Rochester (New York) to get a job caddying there so that he would already be there to caddie for Sam when he got to Rochester to play in the (1956) Open. But the USGA wouldn't allow this. Now, you can bring your caddie anywhere.

Dave Marr:

Sam had a tendency to look in your bag to see what club you were playing. One time we were paired together and we came to a par-three. I had the honor, and I noticed Sam watching me to see what club I pulled. Why Sam Snead would watch *me* is something I still don't understand, but anyway I pulled out a four-iron for a seven-iron shot and then just dead-handed it. The ball came off the clubface like a bag of mush and wound up on the green. Sam looked at me, looked at the yardage, checked the wind, and pulled his five-iron. The ball was still rising when it went over the gallery behind the green. If looks could have killed, the one that Sam gave me would have planted me right on the tee.[2]

Lee Trevino *believes Snead never burned out from playing for money, only that his nerves started to give way:*

There's no telling how many tournaments he would have won had his nerves held out. He probably would have been winning tournaments until he was sixty-five years old. When I beat Jack Nicklaus in the PGA Championship in 1974 in North Carolina, Sam was sixty-two years old and he finished third. He was right there.

Sam was one of those guys who had a tremendous amount of killer instinct. Every time he played, I don't care what it was, he wanted to beat you. I guarantee you he went to his grave looking for a hundred-dollar nassau.

I remember playing a nassau with him one time and beating him. A lawyer friend of mine went down to Port Saint Lucie to play in a pro-am, and Sam was there playing with a Cadillac dealer. We locked horns, and we came to the last hole one up. On the last hole, I pulled my ball over near a palmetto bush. I backed my way into that bush, and all you could see were my arms sticking out. I was pumped, and I hit this ball about 170 yards over some pine trees to about eight feet from the hole. Sam just looked at me and said, "Hey, hey, how did you do that?" We ended up beating them out of twenty-five dollars that day, although I don't remember if we ever got paid. It doesn't make any difference.

George Archer *hadn't been on the PGA Tour long before he got a chance to play with Snead, an opportunity that came along mere minutes after being introduced to him:*

The first time I met Sam was at the Tournament of Champions at Desert Inn in Las Vegas in 1965. I was with Charles Coody and another guy, a first-time winner, whose name I can't remember. We were getting ready to play a practice round. Sam comes along and sees us and asks, "Mind if I join you, boys?" We said, "Sure, Sam, we'd love to have you."

So Sam steps up to the tee and turns toward each of us as he says, "I'll play you five-five-five, you five-five-five, and you five-five-five." I turn around and look at Coody and the other guy, and they don't say anything. So I turn to Sam and say, "Let's play round robin." He says, "What's round robin?" And I say, "We get a new partner every six holes, so each of us gets to have you as a partner for six holes each." Sam says, "Okay, that sounds good. We'll forget the individual stuff." So we got out of the individual stuff.

Sam wins the first team, Sam wins the second team, and the third team was Coody and me. I think Coody birdies the first two holes, so they press us. I birdie the next two holes. Now we've got them four down and two down, with two to play. We go over to the next tee, and Sam don't say nothing. We tee off, and I hit the longest drive. Sam's about ten yards behind me, and Sam's partner is about ten yards behind him, and my partner's over in the lake to the right.

At that point Sam says to his partner, "C'mon, partner, we've got to win this last press." I said, "Sam, are you pressing us out here in the fairway?"

He says, "What do you mean?"

"Well, you didn't press us back at the tee. If you press us in the fairway, it's a two-to-one press."

"What the hell is a two-to-one press?"

"You're putting up ten bucks and we're putting up five bucks because you didn't press us back on the tee."

Sam didn't like that, and he came up to me and kind of got into my face, and I still said, "That's the deal, Sam."

It ended up that we both parred seventeen and we both parred eighteen. Coming off the last green, Sam goes, "How much did I win?" I walked right up to him and got into his face and said, "You didn't win a damn penny, Sam Snead. Thank you very much; we enjoyed the day."

He said, "Okay, boys. I'll see you later." And then he trotted off. From then on, Sam never pulled any crap with me. We got along great. He knew that I liked fishing and hunting. I grew up around Dutch Harrison, another older golfer who had that same mentality. I remember playing with Dutch one time, and Dutch said to me, "When the pros play with the amateurs, the amateurs are supposed to pay up." That was Sam's philosophy: Whoever played golf with him was supposed to pay.

Jack Vardaman*, the Washington, D.C., attorney who became good friends with Snead over the last twenty-two years of Snead's life, often would stay at his second home in Hot Springs. If Snead also happened to be in town, they would get together with other buddies for some golf:*

We had a lot of good games and a lot of good matches. I'm a scratch golfer, and when we started out playing with each other, we played even. I don't think I ever got a stroke from Sam. We played even for a long time, and then in his later years Sam would ask me for strokes. I always told him I would give him strokes only if he wrote on a piece of paper, "I, Sam Snead, asked Jack Vardaman for strokes."

Sam could really play, even at his advanced age. I remember very clearly how at age seventy-one Sam shot 60 at the Lower Cascades (at The Homestead). I had played with him a day or two before and regret not being there to see him shoot the 60, even though it would have cost me a great deal to see it. He shot twelve under par that day and lipped out for birdies on the last two holes.

Vardaman *remembers a time when their foursome at The Homestead also included one of his prominent D.C. neighbors:*

When Dan Quayle was Vice President, he came down one time to play with us at the Cascades Course at The Homestead. The game was that Sam and I would play Dan and another fellow.

In an upset of David-and-Goliath proportions, Dan managed to win ten dollars from Sam. Sam wanted to pay Dan immediately, right as we got off the eighteenth green instead of in front of the people at the clubhouse.

Sam looks in his wallet and all he sees is a twenty. No one had any change, so the Vice President went into the pro shop to get change for the twenty. By the time he came out, there's a crowd around, the Secret Service, and the motorcade. Here comes the Vice President out of the pro shop, and he gives Sam his ten dollars' change.

A lady in the crowd says, "Oh, Mr. Snead. You mean you won money from the Vice President?" Without missing a beat, Sam said, with a twinkle in his eye, "What does it look like?" Nobody in that crowd ever knew that Sam had lost money that day, and Sam liked it that way.

Veteran golfer and CBS golf analyst ***Lanny Wadkins****, like Snead a Virginia native, has long been considered one of the best American match-play golfers in recent history, given his sterling record as a player in Ryder Cup competition. Wadkins recalls a dream come true, getting a chance to play against Snead.*

Sam was my hero growing up. Being a Virginian, I always looked up to him. The first chance I got to play with him was real special. I played with him in a couple of CBS *Golf Classic* matches. We played one match that was taped late in 1973

PHOTO COURTESY OF JACK VARDAMAN

Snead at the Homestead flanked, left to right, by friends David Lee and Jack Vardaman, and Vice President Dan Quayle, who stopped by for a day of golf with the Slammer.

and shown in 1974. It was an individual skins deal where I played against him and Gay Brewer at Firestone Country Club. Gay Brewer shot 69, Sam shot 66, and I shot 63. I won seventeen skins, but to play with Sam Snead was so neat and just getting the chance to watch everything he was able to do. Any chance I had to play with him or be around him, I took. He was a treasure.

One of the neatest things about all this is that I have on video the two CBS matches I played in with Sam, including the one a year earlier, played in 1972, when Jerry Heard and I beat Sam and J. C. in the last team match played in the CBS series. So to have me playing against Sam on film is just something to show the grandkids.

Sam always made me feel very comfortable. When I was a rookie on tour, I came in with the approach that when I played with the legends and icons of the tour, I would call them all "Mister" until they told me not to. But my first day out playing with Sam, he told me right from the start, "I'm Sam." That was it.

Being a Virginian, I had played with him in an exhibition in Richmond when I was about eighteen or nineteen. We always got along well, and we enjoyed the same kind of jokes and humor. He never really offered me much advice, but that's probably because I always played pretty well when I played with him, so there really wasn't much for him to say. I loved playing with him.

I never really had any money games with him in practice. But I did have a great pairing in the 1973 U.S. Open at Oakmont. I played my first two rounds with Sam Snead and Ben Crenshaw. Crenshaw was still an amateur and I was in my second year out on tour. That was a time I'll never forget.

Gary McCord *is on the opposite end of the spectrum from Snead in at least one respect—while Snead holds the PGA Tour record for career victories, McCord is tied with many others for last place, with zero regular tour wins. McCord on Snead:*

I was playing at Disney one time and I was out hitting some balls, and Sam was sort of watching. He was telling me, "You gotta do this, you gotta do that." So I kept working on stuff for about an hour, and then he goes, "Okay, that's good. Now come on over and watch me." And I thought, *Watch you? What could I possibly tell you?* I walked over there and watched him take one swing, and I said, "That looks good, Sam. Gotta go." It was absolutely perfect.

Another time we were playing at Quad Cities, where he shot 66–67 when he was almost seventy years old or whatever. That Saturday I got onto the first green and had about a twelve-footer. I get over the putt, and he starts doing that thing with the change in his pocket. I backed off like I was redoing the putt. I walked around to him and said, "Sam, you don't have to do that to beat me." He looked at me and kind of grinned, and he put the change away.

Johnny Bulla *harks back to the early days of the tour in recalling the hardships of being a club pro on one hand and a touring pro on the other, trying to make ends meet while keeping the bosses happy:*

Sam won two tournaments on the West Coast the first time we went out there together, at Oakland and the Bing Crosby. At the time, he was making forty-five dollars a month plus room and board at his teaching job at The Greenbrier. After he won the tournaments, he went to his boss, a Mr. Johnson, and said, "I think I should be making sixty dollars a month, because I won the two tournaments and earned a little publicity for you." The guy said, "Sam, I'm sorry. But times are tough, and all I can afford to pay you is the forty-five dollars." That's when Sam quit and went out on the tour for good.

Later on, the club brought him back, and this time they gave him carts to be used at the club. But Sam made so much money renting out the carts, he just about killed them. They took the carts away from him, and he quit again. He did come back a third time.

Being a club pro was the only way you could make any money back in those days. There wasn't really any money out on the tour. Everybody had a pro job. You had to. Sam was the first one I knew of that played the tour full-time, although to do that you had to have some backing and endorsements to be able to afford to do it with all the travel expenses involved.

When the day's golf was over, grown men still had to find other competitive ways to occupy the time. ***Bulla****:*

We wrestled some times, just like kids. I was a bit stronger and had about forty-five pounds on him, so I could beat him wrestling.

Doug Ford *gets back on track with golf by talking some more about playing practice rounds with Snead:*

I think I got about as close to Sam as anybody outside of Johnny Bulla. The first time I really got to meet Sam was when I won the tournament at Jacksonville and he finished second. From then on, we played a lot of practice rounds together because he liked my five dollars. Guys used to say to me, "Why do you play with that guy? He's too tough." I'd say, "Well, you've got to pay for an education, and I'm getting a hell of an education out of it."

Sam, Goalby, and I must have played at least seventy-five rounds together at the Masters, practice rounds. I even beat him to win the Masters one year (1957). We were always pretty close in the big tournaments. I played with him in the two first rounds of the U.S. Open won by Jack Fleck (1955), which Sam should have won. The last round got him.

The one Senior Tour event that I won was at Newport, Rhode Island, where I beat him in a play-off. They have a rule now that guys in a play-off can't split (secretly agree to split the combined money from the top two payouts regardless of which one wins), but I asked Sam if he wanted to split that one and he said, "Sure." I then said, "Do you want to play for something?" And he said, "No, let's just split it." That was big money to us, with something like eighteen or twenty thousand dollars going to the winner, when back on the regular tour I don't think we ever got more than twenty-five hundred for winning an event.

Just to show you, the very next week I got into a play-off with Billy Casper. I said the same thing to him, but he said, "Ah, I don't split." Different guys from different eras. The old-timers would split.

***Al Besselink**, himself a legendary gamer in Snead's class, saw Snead as frugal yet generous:*

Sam never threw his money around, but he would never ask you to pay for anything or to leave the tip. He always took care of things.

Bob Hamilton and Dutch Harrison were two of the great players who traveled together. They told me about the time they were in Portland, Oregon, I think it was, and they were hustling people for twenty-five cents. That was in the early days when *nobody* had any money. So here comes Sam Snead, and he says, "Do you mind if I play along?" They only had three, so they said, "Sure, that would be fine. We're just playing twenty-five-cent syndicates." Well, Snead shot like a 64 or 65 and beat them out of four or five dollars.

The next day, when Sam approached them to play some more, they said, "Hey, you can go right on through. We don't want no part of you."

Those were the fun days. We had the greatest life in the history of the world. We didn't have any money, but we had all the millionaires, all the CEOs, all the chairmans of the board wanting to be around the golfers.

Don Wade, *on life with Sam Snead down in Florida:*

Sam told me one time that even though he had won many, many tournaments over the years, he had never won a club championship. Of course, a big reason for that was his turning pro when he was so young. Knowing this, Pine Tree, his home course in Boynton Beach, Florida, passed a special rule saying that Sam could play in the Pine Tree club championship. And he won it.

One time I was playing golf down there with Sam, and after we finished we went into the grill to have lunch. There were two guys in there who came over and started talking to us. It turned out that while Sam was in the navy during the war, he was based in San Diego and didn't do much but play golf the whole time he was out there.

These two guys used to play against Sam all the time out in San Diego, and they would play their best ball against his ball. One of them was a plus-three and the other one either a scratch or a plus-one. In all the time they played, they only beat Sam twice. That should tell you something about how well Sam could play.

Afterward, driving back home, Sam stopped at a K-Mart to buy some flowers, and then we headed back to his place.

We get back there and Sam has this tray of flowers, petunias, that he had bought at the K-Mart. As we're walking up to the front door, I see this contraption that looks like it had been made by a twelve-year-old. It's a box with a trap thing on it with an elastic band, like some sort of Rube Goldberg concoction.

I said, "What is it?"

He said, "It's a rabbit trap. Those dang rabbits have been eating my petunias, and now I've got 'em."

"Does this thing really work?"

"Of course it works, I made it myself."

We go into his kitchen, and he opens up the freezer part of the refrigerator. In there he's got these rabbits that he has skinned and which he is freezing. "I give them to the maid," he said. "She likes them."

7

Scattershot Sam

Many facets and dimensions to Sam Snead's life and career can't be neatly tucked into definitive categories. For instance, there are the many tour records, some of which likely will never be broken. Okay, so Tiger Woods might have a shot at the eighty-two career victories if he can stay focused another fifteen years or so and not cut back too much on his playing schedule. But let's see how old Tiger is when he shoots his age in a tour event for the first time or wins the same event for a ninth time.

The year Snead turned sixty-two, in 1974, he enjoyed a year in golf that might be worth a plaque in some hall of fame. He lost the L.A. Open by two shots to Dave Stockton, won the Par-Three Contest at the Masters, tied for third in the PGA Championship, and was inducted into the World Golf Hall of Fame.

Four years later he teamed with Gardner Dickinson to win the first Legends of Golf event. A year after that, in 1979, at age sixty-seven, he would become the first player in PGA Tour history to shoot his age in a tour event—twice, in fact, on the same weekend—with rounds of 67 and 66 at the Quad Cities Open. In 1982, just a month shy of his seventieth birthday, he paired with Don January to again win the Legends.

With his play in those early Legends tournaments, Snead was a major factor in the explosion of interest in golf for the fifty-and-overs that led to the birth of the Senior PGA Tour, now known as the Champions Tour. By then, though, he was on the cusp of seventy and not quite able to compete on a week-to-week basis with the fifty-something likes of January, Arnold Palmer, and Miller Barber, the stalwarts of the Senior Tour in its early days.

There are many ways to define Sam Snead's legacy and to credit his contributions to the game, even in scattershot form.

Johnny Bulla*, whose only tour victory was the 1941 L.A. Open, offers this perspective on Snead's place in golf history:*

If Sam had only won the U.S. Open, he would be recognized today as the greatest golfer ever. It's kind of like what happened with (Arnold) Palmer and (Tom) Watson—neither of them ever won the PGA Championship, although they each won each of the other three major tournaments. Palmer and Watson were great golfers, but they weren't the golfer that Sam Snead was in his prime.

People ask me all the time, "How would Tiger Woods stack up against Sam?" I say, "Let me tell you something, if

Sam had the same equipment and the same golf ball that Tiger is playing with today, I guarantee you that Sam would hit the ball as far as Tiger does. I guarantee he would. Sam could hit more greens than Tiger, but Tiger would be able to out-putt him."

Think about it: There's never been a pro who had a long career who was able to keep it going even while going through long periods where he couldn't putt. There's going to come a time where Tiger hits that period, and when he does he's going to be just another player.

So much depends on putting. That's why I couldn't win any majors, because I couldn't putt the ball well consistently enough. I played in fifty-four majors in my career and finished in the top ten twenty times, including a couple of seconds in the British Open and a second to Sam in the Masters (1949), but never won one.

Talk about destiny. In that 1949 Masters, Sam hit his drive at eighteen into the trees on the right, but his ball somehow fell to the left, leaving him a fairly clear shot to the green. If the ball had dropped down just a few more yards to the right, he would have been dead in the trees. Now he was able to cut a shot bending right around the trees, although he cut it a bit too much and the ball ended up on a bank on the right-hand side. He then chipped it in for a three, and he ended up beating me (and Lloyd Mangrum) by three shots.

It didn't bother me a bit. I figured I had played the best I could, and that's all I could do. The only one that bothered me was when I four-putted and then three-putted the last two holes at the 1946 British Open. That really bothered me for a couple days, then it never bothered me anymore.

Henry Longhurst *was one of golf's great voices for many years, whose lyrical prose as a legendary writer translated well to his golf commentary in the early days of television. This is what he once wrote about Snead's putting woes:*

> Sam Snead, whose fluent style has lasted longer than any other man's in the history of the game, was reduced to putting between his legs, croquet-fashion—and he was a total abstainer for years. The croquet putter gave many a golfer, myself included, an extended lease on life, and the banning of it was an act of cruelty to many hundreds of miserable wretches for whom the very sight of a normal putter set their fingers twitching. The ease with which you could line up one of these croquet putters to the hole was quite remarkable. By holding the club at the top of the shaft, and loosely lower down with the right arm stiffly extended, the most inveterate yipper could make some sort of a four-foot putt which would not expose him to public ridicule. We did not ask to hole it; all we wanted was to be able to make a stroke at it, and this we could do. The United States Golf Association not only decided to ban a method which had brought peace to so many tortured souls, but the group let its decision become public before the Royal and Ancient Club of St. Andrews had time to consider it, thus putting the latter in the impossible position of either banning the club or falling out with the USGA. So they banned the club.[1]

Freddie Haas *offers this further analysis of Snead's game, tee to green:*

Golf is a game in which you play to your strength, and one of Sam's strengths was that he hit the ball a little farther than most other players, such as Hogan and Nelson. Also, he hit the ball straight, not trying to work it one way or the other. He was a wonderful lag putter, too. If he had a forty-foot putt, it would be most unusual for him to have more than a foot and a half left for his second putt. Sam and Gene Littler were the best at lagging putts that I have ever seen. I would think that not having many putts in the three-to-six-foot range to save par was very good for his nerves, and it gets pretty nervy out there. He ended up using different putting styles later in his career, because most of us, as we get older, get varying degrees of the yips. Sam was no exception. If Sam had been allowed (by the USGA) to continue using his croquet style of putting, there's no telling how many more tournaments he would have won.

Patty Berg, *one of a number of great women golfers befriended by the great Sam Snead, whether via a golf lesson, partnering with him in a tournament, or joining him for an exhibition match, found the Slammer to be great company:*

Sam was a super guy, one of my best friends. I always enjoyed playing with him very much. We partnered in tournaments a number of times, sometimes playing best ball and sometimes alternate shots—it didn't matter; having a golfer like him as your partner was money in the bank.

Three generations of Snead men: from left, Sam's son Jack Snead, J. C.'s son Jason Snead, Sam, and Sam's nephew J. C. Snead.

We both represented Wilson Sporting Goods, but we also hit it off well because we both liked a lot of different sports and always had a lot to talk about. I played in a lot of exhibitions with Sam, and it was obvious people liked him not only because of his great swing but also because he was just so entertaining.

And he was one of the best teachers in the game. I could ask him any question, and he would give a thoughtful answer. I would sometimes go out to the practice range with him, and that gave me plenty of opportunities to watch him and to ask him about all the different kinds of shots that he played.

He helped me with a lot of things in my own game, such as being square to the target in my stance instead of being too closed or open. He would stand right behind you and watch you swing, and he could always tell you quickly and in just a few words exactly what you needed to do to overcome any problem in your swing. His own swing tempo was so great, and that was one thing he would keep after me to work on. I know he helped Babe Zaharias and some of the other girls as well.

Bob Toski *was seventy-five at the time of this writing, but he had no problem recalling his first exposure to Snead way back in the early fifties:*

I remember the first time I played with him in an exhibition. I was in awe of him because I was just a rookie. We were playing at Blue Hills Country Club in Kansas City. The first hole was a par-four that wasn't too long, but the wind was blowing pretty severely right into our faces, maybe around twenty-five miles an hour.

With my being the young whippersnapper, they gave me the honor going off at the first hole. I drove it down the middle of the fairway, and I hit it pretty damn good. Sam got up, hit his, and when we got down there we could see that his ball really wasn't that much beyond mine, about ten yards.

Sam looks at his ball, then looks at mine, and he says, "Geez, Mouse, you swung so hard at that ball, you had two feet in the air. You were high jumping, and they ought to give you a two-stroke penalty for high jumping." I said, "Sam, my ball is ten yards behind yours and it's right in the middle of the fairway." He said, "Yeah, but you keep high jumping like that, Mouse, and it'll catch up to you, because you can't keep getting both your feet into the air and still expect for that ball to keep ending up in the middle of the fairway."

Golf writer ***Don Wade*** *was new to the world of golf magazines when he got his initiation working with Snead, who was a longtime playing editor for* Golf Digest*:*

My first piece I did for *Golf Digest* in 1978 was one I did with Sam. I believe the headline of the piece was "Take a Playing Lesson with Sam Snead." This was done down in Pinehurst, and what they would do is get a few people out there and have Sam play three or four holes. He'd tell people what he was thinking about, and they would ask him questions. This was before the Senior Tour had started and Sam was still playing the regular tour a little bit.

I had always heard what a difficult person Sam could be, but I found him to be wonderful. We sort of hit it off right from the first. One thing that I'm sure is pretty much true at all the golf magazines is that once you, as a writer, find someone you have a good rapport with, you tended to do all the stories involving that golfer. For example, I did almost all of Amy Alcott's stories while I was on staff at *Golf Digest*.

Sam and I got to know each other well, and we played a lot of golf together. When I went down to Virginia to work on stories with him, I would stay at his house. The most insightful story I have of Sam is the time I went down there to do a particular story, and I don't remember which one it was. He was showing me around the house, and it's a beautiful, beautiful house. It overlooks Hot Springs, the mountains, and what have you, and he had all his Masters stuff, including the crystal, in one room.

We came to what basically was a very large walk-in closet. It had all these games and puzzles in there. I said, "Sam, what are these for?" His youngest son, Terry, who as a young boy had had an illness that had impaired his mental development, had been put in a home. He would come and stay with Sam and Audry for one week in the spring and one week in the fall. When I asked him about the games and puzzles, Sam said, "Those are for when Terry comes here. He isn't quite as quick as other kids, but he is a competitor, and he will play you to the hilt in these games. I would give away everything I have if it would make Terry all right, but I'm so proud of him." And as he was saying this, Sam started to cry.

Wade *saw Snead as a great shotmaker on many occasions:*

Snead was playing in the Crosby one year at Pebble Beach. The weather during one round was particularly difficult, with the wind tearing off the water. When he came to the 107-yard, downhill, par-three seventh hole, play was backed up as players struggled to cope with the horrible conditions. When it was Sam's time to play, he had devised a solution. He putted his ball down the sandy walkway. The ball came to rest at the bottom of the hill. From there, Sam pitched the ball onto the green and one-putted for his par.[2]

Lee Trevino *hadn't yet won his first major, the 1968 U.S. Open, when he had the privilege of meeting Snead:*

The first time I really got to meet Sam Snead was in 1967. I first qualified for the Open in 1966, when Arnold Palmer and Billy Casper had that great shootout. I don't remember whether Sam was there or not. But I hadn't even heard of most of these guys, except for Hogan and Nelson, and that's because they were from Fort Worth and I had grown up around Dallas.

I remember one year when I finished second in Houston and second at Atlanta and then went to Rochester to play in the Open. Somewhere along in there—I don't remember exactly where—I was hitting some practice balls and I was complaining about not being able to get the ball up in the air. Sam was standing not too far away talking to Bob Goalby, who says to Sam, "That guy talks a lot and hits the ball low."

Sam comes over to me and asked me what the problem was. I told him that I couldn't get the ball up in the air. He said, "Son, if you want to get the ball up into the air, you're going to have to release the club and stay behind it." I had always swayed going into the ball—I didn't sway going back, but I swayed into it coming through. That was the first and only golf lesson I ever got from a golf professional.

When people ask me who taught me how to play, I say, "Well, the only one I took a lesson from was Snead, and he really did help me in getting the ball up into the air."

Let's keep the needle on ***Trevino****:*

I remember playing at the Diplomat Club down in Florida, and I drew Sam as a partner in the tournament. We came to one long par-four that was against the wind. I hit driver and then still had to hit three-wood to get to the green—it was about 235 yards. Sam looks at this and pulls a driver out. I said to him, "What the hell are you going to do with a driver here?" He took it and hit it down the right side, with the wind blowing from about eleven o'clock to five, kind of a cross wind.

Anyway, he takes the driver and hits it straight up in the air, with a draw, and puts it twenty feet left of the hole. I see this, put my three-wood back in the bag, and shake my head. I knew right then that as long as I live, as much as I love this game and as much as I play it, I will never be able to hit that shot. You could give me a tee, and I would never be able to hit that shot.

I had to be a creative shotmaker simply because I never hit the ball very far, and I primarily hit the ball from left to right—a hook or a draw was out of the question. Sam is the only man I've ever seen who could hit that shot, a high draw with a driver off the fairway. He had a terrific pair of hands on him.

Johnny Bulla *knew Snead as someone who would sometimes try something new, or, better yet, something old:*

Sam had this hickory-shafted driver he would use—he called it his buggywhip driver, and he would try it out every now and then. He would duckhook with it every time he tried to hit it real hard, and I beat him every time. So he made a deal with Dunlop that allowed him to get his clubs for free with the understanding that he would play well. Henry Picard was already with Dunlop, and one time after we finished a practice round I said, "Henry, why don't you give this guy a driver that has a stiff shaft? He can't hit it with this whippy thing."

Henry said, "Well, I got this one here that's too heavy for me. Why don't you give it to him and let him try it?" That thing turned out to be perfect for Sam, and he ended up using it for twenty-five years, until it finally busted all to pieces and he couldn't use it anymore. At the time, Sam said to Henry, "How much do you want for it?" In those days, you would pay five dollars for a club that came straight from the factory. Henry said, "Five dollars? I'll give it to you. You don't need to pay me anything."

Sam said, "No, I want to pay you." So as tight as Sam was, he gave the five dollars to Henry, made him take it. The next week Sam went up to Oakland and won the tournament. After the tournament, Henry went up to Sam and said, "Sam, I want my driver back." Sam said, "Didn't I tell you? I paid you for it, and you can ask Boo-boo (Bulla)." Then he turned and walked away.

Bob Hope, *telling about the time that he was paired with Snead in the pro-am of one of the early Memorial Tournaments hosted by Jack Nicklaus:*

When Muirfield Village first opened, even the pros had trouble. Ed Sneed told (Nicklaus), "Jack, you've built a house without any windows." Meaning that there was no escape. I was playing in the pro-am with Sam Snead one year when his second shot on the par-five fifteenth hole, a perfect shot right down the middle of the fairway, rolled into a creek. Sam was fuming. "What kind of course have you got here?" he asked Nicklaus. "Some of those holes weren't meant to be." Jack softened it up a little over the years, and today it's a fair and beautiful course, a lasting testimonial to the man who built it.[3]

Tommy Bolt *weighs in on analyzing the pros and cons of Snead's game, and where he stood in the annals of golf history:*

Sam didn't have the greatest *swing*, but he had the greatest *tempo* of any player who ever lived. People were always calling him "Slammin' Sammy Snead," but that wasn't the best part of his game. The best part of his game was around the greens. He chipped it in a couple of times against me one time in a televised match.

He was the best player out of the bunkers; he was the best chipper that I've ever seen; and he was also one of the greatest putters that I've ever seen. The only reason he got a reputation for being a bad putter was when he missed that thirty-inch putt at the 1947 U.S. Open that allowed Lew Worsham to win. The media made Sam out to be a bad putter after that. We've all missed a lot of thirty-inch putts in our careers. With Sam, it got ballooned out of proportion.

Hogan was the closest to having the complete game—he was the best player from tee to green. Hogan was more like Tiger Woods than Sam Snead was. The only bad thing about Sam's game was in how after they made him into "the Slammer," he would try to slam the ball every time he teed it up. That's not the way to play golf because he found himself in the woods and in the rough a lot of times.

Sam wasn't the greatest driver of the ball, even if he was one of the longest drivers that we had on the tour in those days. If he had geared it down a notch and kept more drives in the fairway, then there's no question he would have been the greatest ever. But when you get a name and/or a reputation, like Tiger Woods or John Daly, people are always wanting to see you hit the ball a long way. "C'mon, John Boy, hit it!" and you know Daly will take a cut at it just to satisfy the spectators.

***Larry Dennis**, a former editor with* Golf Digest *and a long-time overseer of that magazine's pro panel, got to work one-on-one with Snead a number of times:*

I did several instructional articles with Sam. Don't ask me what all of them were about, although I do remember one bunker piece I did with him. Sam had a sense of hillbilly to him, but he was very, very sharp.

Whenever we did a piece together, I would have some questions prepared to ask him. I needed for him to give me the fundamentals and the nuances and so forth. Usually, I liked to talk things over with the golfers first and get my questions answered before we would move out for a demonstration and the photo shoot. We would sit down and discuss what we were going to do, so that by the time we got out on the course I had most of the rough text done.

With a photographer present, we would get Sam into the bunker or set up for whatever kind of shot it was, and the photographer would do his thing. Basically, with Sam, or for that matter any of these guys, you had to be prepared. You have to know what questions you want to ask. Sam was always very good, very easy to work with. He had a pretty good temper, but he never displayed it around me. We got along famously and became pretty good friends.

He was quite talkative when we sat down to talk for these pieces; he would go on and on. He would recall, in this case, particular bunker shots that he had hit at key times in tournaments. Sam was loquacious, no question about it. He was a natural when it came to the golf swing, so when he talked about it, he wasn't real technical. Even though he didn't get into the technicalities, he always had some key thoughts that he could express quite well and which made a lot of sense.

I did a book with Byron Nelson back in the middle seventies, and it was the same kind of thing in that we would sit down and I would ask him a lot of questions. Byron was great at painting word pictures. Like if you're in a bunker, you want to hit the shot like you're peeling an apple, slicing under the ball. That sort of thing.

Sam wasn't quite like that, but he offered some nice keys, like "At impact, you want to return to your address position." It doesn't really quite work out that way, although if you look at Sam's swing he was pretty close. A lot of times, though, he would essentially say, "I just do it. Don't ask me how." And I'd say, "Sam, that won't help us with the article." You kind of had to pull it out of him, although you really didn't want him to be too technical.

***Dennis** explains the pro panels:*

They were pretty structured, and we had a list of topics about teaching and playing that we would discuss. Out of that, we would develop articles for the magazine. We would go around the room and allot a certain number of minutes for everyone to contribute. But people like Sam would just get to talking, and he was so fascinating that you didn't want him to stop; you were reluctant to interrupt him. It was fun.

***Dennis** started working for* Golf Digest *in 1972, although he had seen Snead in action more than two decades earlier:*

I was in charge of our pro panel, which consisted of teachers and players, one of which was Sam. I hadn't actually met

Sam before then, although I had first seen him in 1948 at the Sioux City Open in Iowa. I must have been a sophomore in high school when I went up there with my dad to watch the tournament.

I'm pretty sure it was the fourth and final round, and Sam didn't seem to be playing that well although he finished third in the tournament. I saw him miss a ten-foot putt on one green, after which he spun his feet around. Of course, they weren't wearing soft spikes back then, and he put a couple of good-sized gouges in the green. He walked off the course saying, "If I make any money in this tournament, just send it to the First National Bank back in White Sulphur Springs in West Virginia" or whatever the bank was. He ended up getting fined a hundred dollars by the tour, which was a lot of money back in those days.

There were times that ***Bob Goalby*** *and other of Snead's pals would do little things to tease their favorite legendary playing partner:*

One time we were playing a friendly match with Sam before a tournament. We paid a photographer to shadow us and snap some pictures. We knew he didn't like playing with photographers around shooting their cameras all the time. That ticked him off, especially back in the fifties and sixties when the cameras were really loud and guys would take shots right in the middle of the backswing.

Doug Ford was just the opposite. He was the best of all time at not letting anything bother him—not a bird, a car, a person, or a dog. You could walk right behind him when he was swinging, drop a club into the bag, or even get in your cart and start it up while he was swinging, and it wouldn't faze him in the least. That helped him be the competitor that he was.

When you're in a tournament, you can get something to bother you on every shot if you go to find it, like somebody moving or a club dropping in another guy's bag and hitting against another club or a squirrel running across the fairway. Something will always bother you if you let it, and that's one of the biggest things guys have to learn in playing the tour—how not to be distracted. But now you see guys telling somebody not to move when they're standing behind the green—two hundred yards away. I know Ford once said that if he had caddied for Sam, he could have won another hundred tournaments. Hogan said the same thing. If Snead had had Hogan's or Nicklaus's composure over shots, he would have won another seventy-five tournaments.

Larry Dennis:

I don't remember exactly what year it was, but I remember watching Sam at Greensboro one time when he was in his sixties. I found him on the practice green, and he was putting the conventional way. He was making everything. I said, "Sam, you're doing pretty good." And he said, "I know, but I can't take it out on the course."

Dennis *again goes back a bit further in time to flesh out the Snead legend:*

I was covering golf for the *Minneapolis Tribune* back in 1957 as a cub reporter right out of school, and I was covering the

Saint Paul Open at a municipal course. I was standing around the practice green one morning, and Jackie Burke Jr. was putting for quarters with Sam. They were putting like twenty-five- and thirty-footers, and at one point Burke yelled over to Mike Souchak, who was on another part of the putting green, and said, "Sutch, how'd you like to know that one out of every three times you set up to a putt like this, you were going to make it?" That's exactly what Sam was doing.

Sam was one of the best long putters in the game, ever. He got a reputation as a bad short putter because he missed that short putt to lose the U.S. Open to Lew Worsham, but he was a great long putter, even though he really wasn't a bad short putter either.

Gary Player *offers a look at Snead from several angles:*

I remember him telling me that he used to practice in his bare feet a lot. That would teach him how to keep his balance. Without those spikes and shoes to support him, he had to stand there and be aware of his great balance.

I admire him because he was not insular in his thinking: he did not want to just play in the United States. He wanted to travel around the world like Nicklaus and Palmer and Trevino and Watson would, and he traveled everywhere to play golf. While Byron Nelson was one of the greatest golfers in America, he certainly wasn't an international golfer.

Sam had a great sense of humor. He was an extraordinary man. Above all, he had a great quality of life. He loved his golf and he practiced as hard as most people practiced, yet he also loved fishing and he loved hunting.

***Freddie Haas** remembers the pleasure of watching Sam practice:*

One day at the Saint Paul Open, all of a sudden I noticed somebody out on the back part of the golf course doing something, although I wasn't exactly sure what it was at first. I turned to someone and said, "What's going on out there? It looks like someone is hitting some shots or something." Sure enough, it was Sam out there.

I went out there to see him and asked what he was doing. Sam turned to me and said, "Have you ever been able to go out to the practice range and hit some shots without having a bunch of people trying to talk to you, asking you how to hit this or how do you do that? I decided to come out here with my caddie and practice some shots, hoping that there wouldn't be too many people coming out to bother me. I never have any peace and quiet when I'm practicing."

Sam liked the attention, but not all the time. It's all right to have the crowd there by the first tee before you tee off. He had no problem with that. But when you really want to work out and perhaps go through all your clubs, you can't do that when you're around too many people.

***Don Wade**, on co-authoring* The Lessons I've Learned, *one of Sam's many books:*

At the time, Sam was being represented by a guy in Los Angeles named Ed Barner, who called me up and said that Sam wanted to do this book and wanted to know if I would do it with him. It was an easy book for me to do because I had already spent a lot of time with Sam and had done a lot of instruction stuff with the magazine that could be adapted for the book.

He was great to work with. We would sit down and he would just talk. Then when it was over, he read through the manuscript, made a few changes, and that was it.

Mark Fry, *director of golf schools at The Homestead, fondly recalls Snead's willingness to surrender some time to the awestruck students who came through there:*

Sam would come up with Meister, his original golden retriever. They were best friends. I think Sam was lonely in his later years. People had the impression that he was gruff and hard to approach. When I was up there at the golf school, working with fifteen to twenty students, Sam would come up there driving his golf cart, and the whole class would just stop what they were doing to stare at him, the legend. Still, everyone was a little apprehensive as they would gather around him, but I would get him to start telling stories. He would then have his photo taken with the students, and they would later send them to him to get them autographed, and he would sign them and send them back.

Sam was hungry for conversation and people, maybe even an acknowledgment at that point. At this point in life, he still wanted to be noticed and he still wanted to talk to people. There would be many situations where he would give the students some help. You can imagine what it had to be like, attending a three-day golf school at The Homestead, and suddenly you're getting a thirty-minute lesson from Sam Snead. He didn't ask for anything in return—it wasn't like

PHOTO COURTESY OF MARK FRY

Snead with two of his best pals: Mark Fry and Snead's beloved golden retriever Meister.

he wanted any money. He wanted to be social and he loved to talk golf, and we became great friends because of that.

Whenever he came up there and I didn't have a golf school going, I'd go right up to the tee with him and talk to him while he hit balls. Even when his eyesight started failing late in life, he would hit on off to the right, and he knew right where it was going as soon as he hit it because he would call it.

When he lost Meister, his dog, he took that very hard. One time soon after that, he had tears in his eyes when he was talking to me about losing Meister, saying he felt like he had just lost a child. After the death of Audry, I think Meister became not only his partner but also his soul mate. The new dog, after Meister, became Buddy, a young, ambitious golden retriever that, when Sam got him, needed to be trained. The first couple times Sam brought him out there,

Sam had Buddy on a short leash. Buddy always liked to chase the ground squirrels, so when one would run by, Buddy would jump off the cart, only for Sam to give him a little jerk. Sam had such a way with animals that it wasn't any time—maybe two or three trips out there—that Sam had Buddy trained well enough to be out there with no leash. While they probably never became the friends that Sam and Meister had been, they became very close friends as well.

You probably also heard about Sam's pet fish. He told me that story about a hundred times. He had a bass that he could just stick his hand into the water, wiggle his finger, and it would come to him. He would then pick it out of the water, pet it and rub it, and then set it back into the water. There was a relationship there that nobody will ever understand.

The Senior PGA Tour, now called the Champions Tour, was launched in 1980 with just two tournaments and purses totaling $250,000. By 2002 it had grown to a major sports entity with a total slate of forty-two events offering more than $63 million in prize money. Snead's total take from playing the Senior Tour was little more than pocket change, but his part in giving the young Senior Tour credibility was significant. ***Gary Player****:*

Sam played an important role because he went to some of the dinners and was always there to help promote it.

Freddie Haas*:*

If it hadn't been for Sam, we probably would have taken longer in getting the Senior PGA Tour started. We had been very concerned back when Sam cut back on his playing in tournaments (in the early fifties), because it was at about the same time that Hogan and Nelson quit playing the tour full time. Sam kept on a little longer, and he was always a terrific draw. He made the Senior Tour considerably more popular than it would have been otherwise. When he won the Legends with Gardner Dickinson, that drew a lot of attention and made the tournament an instant success. Sam was a wonderful competitor who enjoyed a really good match, especially when he won, and he won more than anyone else.

Al Besselink *talks about building a foundation for what would become the Senior Tour:*

I had an office in Orange County with a buddy of mine. We had built the first cordless telephone, but we didn't have the money to pursue it, and look at how big it's gotten. It just goes to show you how big everything is.

Anyway, one day I was watching TV and saw two former football teams having a tug of war in Hawaii for $100,000. I got to thinking what a great idea that was and how it could be translated over to golf. I could get the senior golfers and put on a golf tournament where they could use carts, play easy courses, let them shoot low scores, get a lot of publicity, and we could really do great. My buddy said that's a good idea, but how are we going to do it? I said we needed to get somebody with money and go from there.

I looked in my little book and saw Frank Stranahan's name and number in New York. I hadn't talked to him in something like ten years, so I called that number and he answered the phone. He said, "Bessy, where have you been?" You see, Frank was one of my buddies. In our life all we did was gamble and bet. Stranahan had all the money, so he would lend me whatever I want and then split the winnings. He was another one of the greatest human beings in golf. He did so much for golf, but all people would do is knock him because he was the millionaire playboy. He helped more people, often giving money to people who worked for him, but never wanting them to know where it came from. That's just the way he was.

In talking to him, Frank told me to call Jim Lewis with Champion Spark Plugs. So I called Jim, and he answered the phone. I told him about my idea for a golf tournament for seniors and he said that sounded great. He said, "Give me your phone numbers and all the other information, and I'll get back to you within a couple of days." Well, he called me back two hours later, saying he had gotten two guys to put up $100,000 for four tournaments. Now that's pretty good, considering that in my day, I would play in a tournament at Pinehurst in which the purse for the whole tournament was $5,000.

As it was, I was playing golf with (actor) Jim Garner all the time out at Riviera. He's a great guy and could really play golf—he once shot a 69 and beat me out of two hundred bucks. I told Jim about the idea, and he gave me Bob Hope's number, and we all know how much Bob loves golf and the golfers. So I called Bob Hope, got ahold of him, and I asked him if he had any Sundays available in the next month. He gave me a choice of two, so I picked one to put on an exhibition.

At that point, I called Sam Snead back in West Virginia and told him, "Sam, I need you for an exhibition." He said okay and flew out, paying his own airfare and expenses, and we put on this exhibition to kick off one of the first senior golf tournaments ever put on. We played one of these senior tournaments in California, one in Indianapolis, one in Kansas City, and one other place I can't remember.

Bob Toski *said it was the instant success of the Legends of Golf, the brainchild of Fred Raphael, that paved the way for the Senior PGA Tour:*

I remember when Fred Raphael told us before the first Legends that they might not have enough money to pay us guys. At that time there was no television and the money had to come from the gate. If there weren't any gate receipts, then we wouldn't be getting any cash. He told us that up front, and Demaret said, "Heck, we're going to play anyway." And Demaret was the one who brought the Legends to Onion Creek (outside Austin, Texas).

Fred asked me, "Who do you want to get paired with?" I said I'd like to play with (Gene) Sarazen, because I was an admirer of his. I was told that we would be going off in the first foursome, and when I got to the first tee, I could see spectators lining both sides of the fairway from tee to green. I turned to Gene and said, "I think we're going to get paid."

What really started the Senior Tour was that big Legends play-off we had with something like four or five groups, and this was a five-hole play-off in which they birdied every hole. That was on national television and they electrified the world. That's what captured the imagination of the American public. It wasn't just Sam Snead, although he was instrumental in helping the Senior Tour grow once it got started.

Arnold came along later and gave it a spark, but he had nothing to do with the initial success of the Senior Tour. It made Arnold successful, and I get tired of all those writers and hero-worshippers who give Arnold all the credit. Don't ever ask Tommy Bolt about Arnold Palmer getting the Senior Tour going—he'll give you an earful.

Tommy Bolt *was part of a winning team, with Art Wall, at the Legends of Golf while in his sixties, in 1980, which brings up the subject of physical fitness and Snead. Bolt:*

Sam kept himself in good shape for most of his life. Sam just loved to play in tournaments. He played in almost every tournament that he could, for some reason or another. It kept him going. If you're going to retire, you're going to drop dead. You just got to keep on going and have something to do every day.

Bob Goalby *laments the fact that efforts to get Snead's biggest rival from a bygone era, Ben Hogan, to play in at least one Legends of Golf never paid off:*

We were down at the Masters, and, of course, this was after Hogan had stopped playing in the Masters. Hogan would always arrive in the afternoon of the day of the Champions Dinner and leave the next morning.

Ben came to the club with his coat and tie on, and it was about four o'clock. He came down into the locker room, and

Two masters of their domains—Sam Snead and Jackie Gleason.

I was there with Doug Ford. We said to him, "Why don't you play in the Legends with us, Ben. It would really be nice." He said that his game wasn't for display and he wasn't going to play. Then we mentioned something else a little later on, about all the fun we had playing in the Legends, and we said, "C'mon, Ben, you ought to play with us." And he beat the top of the table with his hand and said, "God d--- you, I told you I wasn't going to play and that's *it*." Yeah, he got mad.

Then at the dinner that night, and this was when the Senior Tour was just getting started, Ben got up and said a few words, and it was nice. And he said, "And I'm not going to play any senior golf. I'm going to leave that to Snead." Sam then blurts out, "I'm going to play 'em *all*, Ben."

I really think Ben would have enjoyed it if he had gotten out there and given it a try. I don't think he knew what it was. Jimmy Demaret wanted Ben to play with him in the first couple of Legends, and I'm surprised that Ben didn't take him up on the offer because he liked Jimmy. But Ben was kind of shy, and he was a bit embarrassed about his game. It wasn't as good anymore, but it was still pretty good, I can assure you of that. It hadn't been that many years that he had shot that 30 at the Masters. In playing the best-ball format of the Legends, he wouldn't have to worry about being embarrassed.

8

Sam I Am: In His Own Words

Sam Snead wasn't exactly a wordsmith, and his public speeches didn't have the polish of a Dale Carnegie or even a Lou Holtz. He could be quite funny in a Richard Pryor sort of way, with censors always standing by to make the jokes printable for daily consumption by the masses.

Snead probably wasn't smooth or analytical enough for a second career as a television golf commentator, and his B.S. wasn't up to the snuff of being able to stretch what should have been a ten-second golf tip into a sixty-second infomercial. When you consider Snead's supposedly hillbilly roots and his self-awareness in that regard, you might have thought him capable of being the Yogi Berra of golf, turning self-deprecating malapropisms into a cottage industry. But that wasn't Snead's style.

Snead was refreshing for his candor and ability to cut to the chase. He could think quickly on his feet, turning an off-the-cuff remark into the perfectly timed rejoinder to an innocent or naíve remark from a bystander.

It got to be old (straw) hat with Snead that somewhere along the line he would be mistaken for a Ben Hogan or a Gay Brewer. But he took it all in stride, always ready with a quip that would entertain and not insult. Had Snead ever chosen to become a standup comic doing the club circuit, you could bet your bottom dollar that he would have been more than capable of shutting up hecklers in the peanut gallery, scorching a few ears along the way.

On his childhood in rural Virginia:

We never wore shoes until it snowed.[1]

On his inability as a youth to sit still for very long:

I used to skip Sunday school because I hated sitting in one place for all that time.[2]

On Christmas, while growing up in Virginia:

The only time I didn't much like was Christmas. I wasn't able to give everybody presents, on account of we were so poor. We didn't get much either. I'd go down and play with the toys the other kids got.[3]

On the strength of his mom, Laura, who gave birth to Sam when she was forty-seven:

A barrel of flour weighed 192 pounds, and Mom would roll it up on her leg and somehow put it right up in a wagon.[4]

On seeing for the first time the Pete Dye-designed course at Harbour Town, with all its railroad ties and bulkheads:

It's a nice course. But it's the first course I ever saw that could burn down.[5]

On seeing the Old Course at St. Andrews prior to the 1946 British Open:

Look yonder at that farm there. It looks like that might have been an old golf course that's gone to seed.[6]

Addressing the age-old rumor of what he used to do with his money, instead of taking it to the bank:

Jimmy Demaret started this story about me burying my money in tomato cans out in my backyard. I never thought anyone would take it seriously until my wife called me at The Homestead one night and said there was some guy out digging up the backyard.[7]

On his ability to read people, mostly his opponents on the golf course:

You watch for little yingy-yangy things in opponents, changes in mannerisms. When I was a teenager, I worked in Doc Ridgeley's drugstore in Hot Springs, Virginia, and I learned to read people. An ole boy would come in and say he'd pay his bill Saturday, but he said that two Saturdays ago.[8]

On his longevity as a professional golfer, covering seven decades:

One reason I've been able to play so long is that I've kept my hand in it. If I had taken two weeks off without touching a club it would have taken me a month to get my game back, which is what most so-called weekend players don't understand. They think golf's a game you can just lay down and pick up like a favorite rifle. I went on a safari to Africa one time. To keep my swing in shape I used to play the other guys for a little money. We didn't have any balls, so we'd play with animal droppings. I had the edge though. When my brothers and I were kids we'd hit horse droppings because what balls we could find we'd sell over at The Homestead. The trick is to hit them on the dried-out side. I knew that, but the other guys didn't, so theirs would keep breaking. They never did figure it out.[9]

On how aging golfers can keep playing well:

To be successful in senior golf, keep the desire to win. If you put a few dollars on a game when you were younger, keep doing it. Don't pad your handicap, either. Force yourself to play your best and hardest, and play every day. If you'd rather putter than putt, it's all over for you as a golfer.[10]

Giving swing advice to President Dwight Eisenhower after Ike complained about losing distance off his tee shots:

Well, Mr. President, you're not turning. You've got to get your ass into the shot.[11]

On luck vs. skill:

I always tried to make my own luck, you know?[12]

On his independence:

I just liked living by my own wits and depending on myself for a win.[13]

On one of the lessons he gave while the pro at The Greenbrier, in White Sulphur Springs, West Virginia:

I tried to teach him my stroke, and that forced me to think about it and to break it down into parts. Except the real secret was, there were no parts. It was pretty much all one motion. I told him that I'd hum a tune and use the rhythm of the music to time my swing so it came out naturally. I also realized that I led with my hips, and I used my feet as anchors for every shot I made. I found that if I rolled my right foot just a little bit and let the power come from there, I was about as rooted as an old pine tree and could put that power right behind the ball.[14]

On his self-perception:

My hillbilly background provided golf writers with plenty of grist. . . . I don't think I was ever totally the rube they made me out to be, but they loved to hear about how I'd spend time between tours back up at Ashwood with my folks. My roots were up in those hills, and no matter how my career was getting along I found I couldn't stay away from home too long.[15]

On the joy of golf and how it pertains to pressure:

Playing golf is fun, and learning how to play it in the public eye is one of the most fun things. Doing well is very satisfying, but doing well in front of a crowd—there's nothing like it. I didn't feel the pressure of being what you might call a star. I don't really know what the hell it was. It used to mean something different than it does today. It was bigger in the sense that you had to do more to get it, but it was also smaller in the sense that the circle of real intense fans was till pretty limited. Still, they'd be taking pictures of you with a pretty girl, and you'd think, Well, geez, this is pretty good. I enjoyed it.[16]

On the early days of competing on tour, when purses were small and there was great pressure just to break even, with expenses:

I remember some of the boys would be leading the first day; they would go out and get drunk at night and say, "I can't do any better than that."[17]

On golf's place in the sporting world:

I that believe golf, not horse racing, is the true sport of kings. It attracts powerful and talented people from all walks of life like no other sport ever has or can. There are no teams as such, and it's a one-on-one sport, so all kinds of special folks get involved. Tending to be pretty easygoing on the course, telling jokes on the way in and such, I found myself attracting some surprising—for me—playing partners.

In the twenty years after (World War II), this country boy, who learned golfing in the Black Creek Mountains with my pals Piggie McGuffin and Horsehair Brinkly, had the honor of playing with nearly every celebrity, from Bob Hope to the King of Windsor—see what I mean about the "sport of kings"? Golf also, especially since Eisenhower, is the sport of presidents, and I've found myself teeing it up with Ike, Nixon, and Jerry Ford.[18]

On comparing golf to baseball:

One day I was talking to Ted Williams in the dugout before a Red Sox game. Some of the Sox were kidding me about the soft life of a professional golfer. Williams said, "Now, you use a club with a flat hitting surface and belt a stationary object. What's so hard about that? I have to stand up there with a round bat and hit a ball that's whizzing by too fast for most people to see it."

"Yeah, Ted," I told him, "but you don't have to go up in the stands and play all your foul balls. I do."[19]

On one of golf's hidden dangers:

I was in a pond in Florida with my boots and ballgetter, fishing around in the water for balls. I had one foot on dry land, the other in the pond. So I'm looking around in the water and what do I look down to see? There's an alligator *right there*, within two feet of my foot. It wasn't a tremendous alligator, but he eased right up to me with his mouth open. Those things can run like hell, but that day I ran faster.[20]

On the game of golf:

Golf is two games, played in two ways and in two places. The first game is played by hitting your ball through the air. The second is played by rolling your ball on the ground. Some people have the nerve and the ability to roll it on the ground. It doesn't take any strength to speak of, but it takes mind, concentration, and muscle control.[21]

On effort:

In golf, you get out of it what you put into it. Most people won't put much into it.[22]

On the golf swing:

The golf swing is mainly something that's learned—a habit you must acquire. Acquiring it is hard work; at least it was for me. Maintaining it is just as hard.[23]

On having the yips in his later years:

I was a wrist putter, and I got the yips quick. When you get to using the fine muscles, you're apt to get a little jick or wiggly-woggly.[24]

On playing a course for the first time:

When playing a strange course, I find it helps to walk some fifteen or twenty paces ahead of my ball and look at the scene from there. This perspective gives you a better idea of where the flagstick sets on the green. It also makes you aware of any hidden depressions along the way that might make the shot look shorter than it really is.[25]

On the Rules of Golf:

The rules exist not only to explain your duties as a golfer, but also your rights. There are many times when these rights can actually help you shoot a lower score, or beat an opponent. . . . Close study of the rules will not only prove rewarding in terms of helping your scoring and increasing your status around the club; it will also give you a much deeper understanding and appreciation of the game.[26]

On preparing to hit a shot:

Shortening your time over the ball before swinging will improve your shots on two accounts. First, you'll swing with greater freedom and better rhythm because of reduced muscle tension. Second, your whole approach to your shots will be more positive. You'll have eliminated all that time over the ball that you once gave to thinking about how you might miss it.[27]

On the pace of a golf swing:

Starting the club back slow sets the pace for your swing. A slow start leads to a longer swing arc because you can continue to hold the club lightly. A fast start makes you increase your grip pressure to control the club. This tightening stifles the length of your backswing.[28]

On Ben Hogan:

I'd never watch Ben swing because his tempo was so much faster than mine that I was afraid it might throw me off. People have tried to say I didn't watch Ben because I didn't like his swing. That's not true. He had a good swing, and it worked just fine for him. It was just a question of tempo.[29]

On golf's elusive nature:

Nothing ever stays the same in golf. Just when you think you've got it all figured out, the game jumps up and reminds you that you haven't begun to figure it all out.[30]

On his athleticism:

I was always a pretty good athlete. I just naturally enjoy competing and the pressure that comes from being in contention.[31]

On finding another mark:

I may have played in more pro-am events than anyone else alive. And it's a safe bet that I've studied more amateurs over a five-dollar nassau than you could shake a stick at. After all these years I totally agree with the old saying that there's no prettier sight on the first tee than an opponent with a fast backswing and a fat wallet—the faster and fatter the better.[32]

On his nephew J. C. Snead:

J. C. might have been better off if his name had been Smith. That way, people wouldn't spend as much time comparing the two of us.[33]

On dealing with mistakes:

Golf is a game of mistakes. Nobody hits every shot perfectly. Nobody gets all the luck running his or her way. But the players who get the most from their games are the ones who make the smallest mistakes—and the smallest number of them.[34]

On gamesmanship:

I've never believed much in giving the needle. It seems to me that it's more bother than it's worth, and your time and energy is better spent.[35]

On throttling back in match play:

Longer hitters always have an edge, but there are times when I'll deliberately lay up off the tee so I'll be away and hitting first. I figure that if I can cozy a shot in there close, there's just that much more pressure on my opponent.[36]

On golf equipment:

As I've said a thousand times, you can't go into a (golf) shop and buy a good golf game. No matter how much God-given talent you might have, you're only going to get as much out of the game as you put into it. That's not to say you can't place a down payment on a better game by investing in some equipment that is suited, not only to your game, but also to the course you're playing.[37]

On road trips in the tour's early days:

Driving through west Texas at night, there were times you didn't need to turn your headlights on. If there were no clouds and the moon was full, you could see the road just fine. The only thing you had to worry about was running out of gas. That, and those big dips in the road. When it rained, they filled with water, and if you hit one you could wreck your car.[38]

On the time he passed two cars in Florida at 110 miles per hour:

The first car was a policeman, and he was chasing a speeder.[39]

On August National Golf Club and Masters Tournament co-founder Clifford Roberts:

Cliff was a tough b------, but you have to be to run that place. The caddies there think his death was a murder, not a suicide, and I believe them.[40]

On Bobby Jones:

A good driver, good fairway wood player, and good around the greens. Not a very good iron player, though. The field lapped him on the par-threes.[41]

Photo courtesy of Suzie Snead

Sam and his nephew J. C. Snead came to enjoy each other's company, whether at the practice putting green or at home in Virginia over dinner.

On his pet bass:

At first he let me tickle his belly, then he got to where he would lay across my hands and let me scoop him out of the water. I don't know why, but he liked being out of the water.[42]

On his legendary memory for golf shots:

Two guys came up to me not long ago and said they saw me hit the greatest shot I ever hit, at New Orleans. I asked 'em if it was off a ditch bank. Yeah. Par-five? Yeah. Cut a three-wood six feet from the hole? Yeah. Missed the putt to the right? Yeah. They couldn't believe I remembered all that.[43]

On growing up during Prohibition and being around country stills:

I didn't drink till I was fifty, and it's a good thing. They'd put anything in that whisky—tobacco, lye, you name it. That stuff would burn the hair off a dog. They had mules on watch to warn 'em the revenuers were comin'. A mule could always hear somebody before you could. When the mule's ears went up, watch out![44]

On his incessant desire to get another money game going, even well into his eighties:

The road's getting shorter and narrower, but I'll play whenever the pigeons land.[45]

On his overseas popularity:

They called me the God of Golf in Japan.[46]

On some advice he once gave a golf student:

Lay off for a few weeks, then quit for good.[47]

On taking it easy:

Take it easily and lazily, because the golf ball isn't going to run away from you while you're swinging.[48]

On his enduring popularity when it came to signing collectibles:

I'll go in the store to sign, and they'll do five thousand dollars worth of business in an hour and a half. People have gone completely nuts over this autograph stuff. I don't get it.[49]

On home, sweet home:

I have the only house I know of that I can sit on the toilet and see a turkey in the backyard.[50]

On the difference between humans and animals:

People are the cruelest thing that walks this earth. You just look at what they do to each other, to animals. Animals don't do that—they kill to survive.[51]

On a case of mistaken identity:

I was in the Waldorf Astoria in New York one time, and a guy is running down the hall yelling, "Mr. Hogan, Mr.

Hogan, can I have your autograph?" I told him I wasn't Mr. Hogan. He said, "Well, you're somebody." And I said, "You'd better believe it."[52]

On his little-known heart problems:

I've had a heart skip since I can remember. My heart'll go pluck, pluck, pluck-uk. Pluck, pluck, pluck, pluck-uk. Then it might go pluck, pluck-uk, pluck. I just hope it keeps on plucking. My doctor told me I had two heart attacks years ago, and I didn't know anything about it.[53]

On the unfulfilled talents of golfer John Daly:

I believe I could take John Daly, if he'd listen, and have him winning.[54]

On what it takes to be successful at golf:

Putting is number one, driving is number two, and being a good wedge player is number three. If you've got a good wedge, you're bodacious.[55]

On what scares him:

I agree with Porky Oliver. He said there were three things he was scared to death of: a downhill, two-foot putt; Hogan; and lightning.[56]

On his treatment by the media:

I had just one story that bothered me. When you come off the eighteenth green, those kids would be right around you, and I'd say, "Now, don't get in front. I might step on your feet with these spikes." And a guy wrote the story up in a Virginia paper. It said, "Snead was his dirty old self. He said to the little kids there, 'If you don't get out of the way, I'm going to step on you.'" A doctor from Roanoke told me about it. He said, "Come on, we'll go and call the desk." I said, "I don't know who the writer is, but if you will have him there, I'll drive to Roanoke, and I'll tell him that he's a damn liar." I never have said that to kids. I love kids. I'd have stopped and signed all day if they wanted.[57]

On life's ebbs and flows:

The sun don't shine on the same dog's tail all the time.[58]

On the Masters Tournament:

I'm proud of the fact that when (Bobby) Jones was asked which was the greatest of all the Masters Tournaments he had seen, he said the Snead-Hogan play-off (in 1954). I could always raise my game another notch or two for Hogan.[59]

On Augusta National:

I couldn't name you five members at Augusta. . . . And I've never been curious to know who they are. But I gave the club my one-iron one time, and it has been displayed, so I know they appreciate me.[60]

On a proper playing weight:

A key to continue winning in the Seniors is to not let yourself get too fat. An overweight golfer, especially an older fella with less flexibility, puts on strokes whenever he puts on pounds. Bobby Jones used to like to take on a few extra pounds before he played in a championship because he felt it gave him something to burn. By the end of the tournament he'd lose all that extra weight plus some more. But Bobby Jones was an unusual man. His kind of metabolism, and self-discipline, is rare.[61]

On how his putting stroke left him over time:

My velvet swing hasn't left me, but putting has always been my weak spot—from the word go. Early on I'd modeled myself on Bob Jones, letting my wrists guide my stroke. That's fine when you're young and you've got your nerves. But when you get a few years past thirty, little things begin to slip, the same little things that help you win golf tournaments.[62]

On copying other swings worth emulating:

As a young player, I would watch other swings very carefully and try parts of swings I liked to see if they fit with mine. Usually, I ended up discarding the new piece, but it was fun to see what I could invent in my "laboratory."[63]

On the one bad club in his bag:

I did have problems with my seven-iron, though, and to this day I can't figure it out. I'd hook that thing, and I'd beat it on the ground. I'd bend it to adjust the lie angle; I did everything to the club you could think of to try to get that hook shot out of it. I mean, I wouldn't hook the six-iron or the eight-iron, but that seven-iron. . . . It could have been the shaft, because I never did switch it. A lot of times, I'd hit a hard eight or an easy six. I'd play around it and wouldn't even use the seven.[64]

On pacing himself:

I was aware of my breathing, and, when it got shallow and fast, I knew I needed to slow down. The more you are in tune with your thinking and with what your body is doing, the better you are able to control your swing. This sensitivity that I had to what I was feeling and thinking helped me perform better. I'm sure of it.[65]

On focus:

I have always felt that you could have all the talent in the world, but if you can't focus you won't come anywhere near achieving your potential in golf. Once you get on the course, it's all concentration.[66]

On what he once told Bob Hope about putting, according to Hope:

Sam Snead once gave me a valuable putting tip. "Don't worry about the line; think more about the distance," Sam said. "Most of the three-putting I see results from stroking the first putt either four feet short or four feet long. Try to get a good feel for the distance to the hole." Easy enough for Sam to say.[67]

NOTES

Chapter 1:

1. Snead, Sam, with George Mendoza, *Slammin' Sam*. New York: Donald I. Fine, 1986, pp. 28-29.
2. Ibid., pp. 32-33.
3. Ibid., pp. 45-46.
4. *Golf World*, May 31, 2002.

Chapter 2:

1. Snead, Sam, with Fran Pirozzolo, *The Game I Love*. New York: Ballantine Books, 1997, p. 7.
2. Ibid., p. 8.
3. Snead, Sam, with Don Wade, *The Lessons I've Learned*. New York: Macmillan, 1989, p. 12.
4. Towle, Mike, *I Remember Bobby Jones*. Nashville, TN: Cumberland House Publishing, 2001, p.54.
5. Snead and Mendoza, p 150.
6. Penick, Harvey, with Bud Shrake, *Harvey Penick's Little Red Book*. New York: Simon and Schuster, 1992, p. 37.
7. Hobbs, Michael, compiler, *In Celebration of Golf*. New York: Charles Scribner's Sons, 1982, p. 83.
8. Snead and Wade, p. 53.
9. Snead and Pirozzolo, , pp. 32-33.
10. Penick and Shrake, p. 135.
11. Ibid.
12. Nicklaus, Jack, with Ken Bowden, *My Story*. New York: Fireside, 1998, p. 12.

Chapter 3:

1. Snead and Mendoza, p 106.
2. Ibid., p. 96.
3. Snead and Wade, p. 117.
4. Snead and Mendoza, p. 80.
5. *Golf Digest*, April 1999.

Chapter 4:

1. Towle, Mike, *I Remember Bobby Jones*, p.144.
2. Wade, Don, *And Then Jack Said to Arnie . . .* Chicago: Contemporary Books, 1991, p. 171.
3. Snead and Mendoza, p 166.
4. Snead and Pirozzolo, pp. 103-104.
5. Wade, Don, *And Then Arnie Told Chi Chi . . .* Chicago: Contemporary Books, 1993, p. 105.
6. Snead and Wade, p. 32.

Chapter 5:

1. Snead, Sam, with Dick Aultman, *Golf Begins at Forty*. New York: Doubleday, 1978, p. 56.
2. Wade, Don, *And Then Jack Said to Arnie . . .* Chicago: Contemporary Books, 1991, p. 171.
3. Derr, John, *Uphill Is Easier*. Pinehurst, NC: Cricket Productions, 1995, p. 99.
4. Ibid., pp. 100-101.
5. *Golf Digest*, April 1999.
6. Ibid.
7. Snead and Pirozzolo, p. 84.
8. Wade, Don, *And Then Arnie Told Chi Chi . . .* Chicago: Contemporary Books, 1993, p. 46.
9. Towle, Mike, *I Remember Bobby Jones*, p.106.
10. Hope, Bob, *Confessions of a Hooker*. Garden City, NJ: Doubleday and Company, 1985, p. 18.
11. Snead and Pirozzolo, p. 176.
12. *Golf Digest*, April 1999.
13. Ibid.

Chapter 6:

1. Towle, Mike, *I Remember Bobby Jones*, p.98.
2. Wade, Don, *And Then Arnie Told Chi Chi . . .* Chicago: Contemporary Books, 1993, p. 203.

Chapter 7:

1. *The Best of Henry Longhurst*. New York: Simon and Schuster, 1978, p. 80.
2. Wade, Don, *And Then Arnie Told Chi Chi . . .* Chicago: Contemporary Books, 1993, p. 207.
3. Hope, p. 55.

Chapter 8:

1. *Golf World*, May 31, 2002.
2. Wade, Don, *And Then Arnie*

Told Chi Chi . . . Chicago: Contemporary Books, 1993, p. 205.
3. Snead and Mendoza, p. 26.
4. *Golf World*, May 31, 2002.
5. Wade, Don, *And Then Arnie Told Chi Chi* . . . Chicago: Contemporary Books, 1993, p. 204.
6. Wade, Don, *And Then Jack Said to Arnie* . . . Chicago: Contemporary Books, 1991, p. 175.
7. Ibid., p. 179.
8. *Golf Digest*, March 1994.
9. Wade, Don, *And Then Jack Said to Arnie* . . . Chicago: Contemporary Books, 1991, p. 180.
10. Snead and Mendoza, p 185.
11. Wade, Don, *And Then Jack Said to Arnie* . . . Chicago: Contemporary Books, 1991, p. 55.
12. Snead and Mendoza, p. 13.
13. Ibid., pp. 38.
14. Ibid., p. 53.
15. Ibid., p. 74.
16. Ibid., p. 94.
17. *Golf Digest*, July 1996.
18. Snead and Mendoza, pp. 120-121.
19. Ibid., p 135.
20. Ibid., p 143.
21. Ibid., p 205.
22. Snead and Aultman, p. 13.
23. Ibid.
24. *Golf World*, May 31, 2002.
25. Snead and Aultman, pp. 36-37.
26. Ibid., p. 60, 64.
27. Ibid., p. 83.
28. Ibid., p. 107.
29. Snead and Wade, p. 28.
30. Ibid., p. 35.
31. Ibid., p. 51.
32. Ibid., p. 52.
33. Ibid., p. 108.
34. Ibid., p. 113.
35. Ibid., p. 124.
36. Ibid., p. 126.
37. Ibid., p. 139.
38. *Golf Digest*, April 1999.
39. Ibid.
40. Ibid.
41. Ibid.
42. Ibid.
43. *Golf Digest*, March 1994.
44. Ibid.
45. Ibid.
46. *Golf World*, November 29, 1996
47. *The Bathroom Sports Quote Book*. Saddle River, NJ: Red-Letter Press, 1991, p. 17.
48. Ibid., p. 16.
49. *Golf World*, November 29, 1996.
50. Ibid.
51. Ibid.
52. Ibid.
53. Ibid.
54. Ibid.

55. Ibid.
56. *Golf Digest*, July 1996.
57. Ibid.
58. Hagen, Walter, *The Walter Hagen Story* (and excerpted from a 1954 issue of *Life* magazine). New York: Simon and Schuster, 1956, p. 265.
59. Towle, Mike, *I Remember Augusta*. Nashville, TN: Cumberland House Publishing, 2000, p. 139.
60. Ibid., p. 169.
61. Snead and Mendoza, p. 186.
62. Ibid., p. 162.
63. Snead and Pirozzolo, p. 2.
64. Ibid., p. 41.
65. Ibid., p. 83.
66. Ibid., p. 99.
67. Hope, p. 86.

Sam Snead's Tournament Victories

1936

* * West Virginia PGA
* West Virginia Open
* West Virginia Closed Professional
* Virginia Closed Professional

1937

* West Virginia Open
* * Bing Crosby Pro-Am
* * Miami Open
* * Nassau Open
* * Oakland Open
* * Saint Paul Open

1938

* * Bing Crosby Pro-Am
* * Canadian Open
* * Chicago Open
* * Goodall Round Robin
* * Greensboro Open
* * Inverness Four-Ball
* * Palm Beach Round Robin
* * Westchester 108-Hole Open
* * White Sulphur Springs Open
* Saint Paul Open
* Greenbrier Open
* West Virginia Open
* West Virginia PGA

---

* Denotes official PGA Tour victories

SOURCES: *The Game I Love*, by Sam Snead with Fran Pirozzolo; *and Senior* PGA *Tour Media Guide*

1939

* Miami Biltmore Four-Ball
* Miami Open
  Ontario Open
* Saint Petersburg Open

1940

* Anthracite Open
* Canadian Open
* Inverness Four-Ball
  Ontario Open

1941

* Bing Crosby Pro-Am
* Canadian Open
* Henry Hurst Invitational
* North and South Open
* Rochester Times Union Open
  Saint Augustine Pro-Am
* Saint Petersburg Open

1942

  Córdoba Open
* PGA Championship
  Saint Augustine Pro-Am Championship
* Saint Petersburg Open

1943

World War II military service

1944

* Portland Open
* Richmond Open
  Middle Atlantic Open

1945

* Dallas Open
* Gulfport Open
* Jacksonville Open
* Los Angeles Open
* Pensacola Open
* Tulsa Open
  11th Naval Open–San Diego

1946

* British Open
* Greensboro Open
* Jacksonville Open
* Miami Open
* Virginia Open
* World Championship of Golf
  War Bond Open

1948

  Seminole Pro-Am
* Texas Open
  Havana Invitational
  Havana Pro-Am
  West Virginia Open
  West Virginia PGA

1949

* Dapper Dan Open
* Greensboro Open
* Masters Tournament
* PGA Championship
* Washington Star Open
* Western Open
  Capitol City
  Decatur Open
  National Celebrities
  West Virginia PGA
  West Virginia Open

Tournament Victories

1950

* Bing Crosby Pro-Am
* Colonial National
  Invitational
* Greensboro Open
* Inverness Four-Ball
* Los Angeles Open
* Miami Beach Open
* Miami Open
* North and South Open
* Reading Open
* Texas Open
* Western Open
Quarter Century Open

1951

* Miami Open
* PGA Championship
Greenbrier Open
Inverness Round Robin
Quarter Century Open

1952

* All-American Open
* Eastern Open
Greenbrier Pro-Am
* Inverness Four-Ball
Julius Boros Open
* Masters Tournament
* Palm Beach Round Robin
Canadian Open
West Virginia Open
Greenbrier Festival
Seminole Pro-Am
Mid-South Open—Pinehurst

1953

* Baton Rouge Open
Greenbrier Pro-Am
Texas Open
Greenbrier Festival
Orlando Two-Ball
Scranton Open

1954

* Masters Tournament
* Palm Beach Round Robin
Panama Open
Los Angeles Mixed (with
  Babe Didrikson Zaharias)
La Gorce Individual

1955

* Greensboro Open
* Insurance City Open
Miami Beach Open
* Miami Open
* Palm Beach Round Robin
Hartford Open
Bayshore Individual

1956

* Greensboro Open
Boca Raton Open
San Diego Open

1957

* Dallas Open
* Palm Beach Round Robin
West Virginia Open
George Mays World Open

1958

* Dallas Open
Greenbrier Invitational
Virginia Open
West Virginia Open
West Virginia PGA
Normandi Isle Open

1959

Sam Snead Festival
West Virginia PGA
George Mays All-American Open

1960

* De Soto Open
* Greensboro Open
Hecks Open
Quarter Century Open

1961

Sam Snead Festival
* Tournament of Champions
West Virginia Open

1962

Palm Beach Round Robin
West Virginia PGA

1963

West Virginia PGA

1964

Haig & Haig Scotch Mixed Foursome
PGA Seniors Championship
World Seniors Championship

1965

* Greensboro Open
PGA Seniors Championship
Haig & Haig Scotch Mixed Foursome
World Seniors Championship
West Virginia PGA

1966

Sam Snead/Greenbrier Festival
West Virginia PGA
West Virginia Open

1967

PGA Seniors Championship
West Virginia PGA
West Virginia Open

1968

West Virginia Open

1969

El Dorado Professional Member

1970

PGA Seniors Championship
West Virginia PGA
Greenbrier Open
World Seniors Championship

1971

West Virginia Open
PGA Club Professional Championship

1972

PGA Seniors Championship
World Seniors Championship
Los Angeles Senior Championship
West Virginia Open

1973

PGA Seniors Championship
World Seniors Championship
CBS Golf Classic (with Gardner Dickinson)
Newport Seniors Championship
West Virginia Open

1978

Legends of Golf (with Gardner Dickinson)

1980

Golf Digest Commemorative

1982

Legends of Golf (with Don January)

1983

Legends of Golf (with Gardner Dickinson)

INDEX